PENTECOST IN TULSA

The Revivals and Race Massacre that Shaped
the Pentecostal Movement in Tulsa

Daniel D. Isgrigg

Seymour Press ᔆᴾ
Lanham, Maryland

Copyright © 2021 – Daniel D. Isgrigg

All Rights Reserved. No part of the book may be reproduced in any form without written permission from Seymour Press.

Published by Seymour Press 2021
Lanham, Maryland
www.seymour.press

ISBN: 978-1-938373-54-1
LCCN: 2021938090

Printed in the United Stated of America

ENDORSEMENTS

"Daniel Isgrigg's book, *Pentecost in Tulsa* is a healing balm to the black community destroyed in the Tulsa Massacre and an opportunity for a "come to Jesus moment" for the white Christian community. Written from an anti-racist historical perspective, Isgrigg challenges the reader to examine their own complicity and perpetuation of forms of community that impede racial reconciliation within the Christian community in general, Pentecostalism in particular. He deserves to be commended for his moral courage to tread into the painful recesses of Tulsa's history, meticulously excavating its past, and leaving no stones unturned. In a historical moment that finds our nation repolarized around race relations, Isgrigg's study provides a model of truth and conciliation. This is a must read for all who dare to know the truth and be set free."

Dr. Raynard Smith, Associate Professor of Pastoral Care/Pastoral Theology New Brunswick Theological Seminary

"Daniel Isgrigg's exhaustive research has produced a compelling history of Pentecostalism in Tulsa, Oklahoma and its far-reaching impact into the 21st century. He has uniquely and thoughtfully captured the impact of 20th century social culture upon the Pentecostal church and how that impacts our community today. His thoughtful research is a wonderful contribution to the canon of information of Tulsa's history and the impact of the Pentecostal Movement that continues today."

Clifton L. Taulbert, President & CEO of Freemount Corporation
Pulitzer Prize Nominated Author, Once Upon A Time When We Were Colored and Eight Habits of the Heart

"*Pentecost in Tulsa* is a must read for anyone interested in the history of the Spirit-empowered movement, a global phenomenon with over 650 million adherents impacting every nation on planet earth. Yet, the story of this movement is made up of thousands of local communities who have embraced the work of the Holy Spirit and sacrificed much to trumpet the gospel of the Kingdom in their part of the world. Tulsa, considered by many to be the epicenter of the Charismatic movement, is one of those communities that has a very unique story. This book takes you behind the scenes to understand the deep well of spiritual power that was dug out in Tulsa many years ago and the deep need for healing in this community. It also chronicles the events that gave rise to the 20th Century's most prolific healing ministries as well as the leading university in Spirit-empowered Christianity. Dr. Isgrigg has done a brilliant job in pulling together this history into one book. I loved reading it and I know you will too!

Dr. William M. Wilson, President, Oral Roberts University
Chair, Pentecostal World Fellowship and Global Co-chair, Empowered21

"Daniel Isgrigg has captured the story of Tulsa's rich Pentecostal heritage that has gone unheralded until now. His careful research is delightfully inclusive of the many various groups within this Pentecostal family. I highly recommend this to anyone sincerely interested in academic research about Pentecostalism."

Pastor Don Martin, Metro Pentecostal Church Tulsa, OK
Chairman, Pentecostal Heritage Society of United Pentecostal Church International

Table of Contents

Preface i

Chapter 1: Introduction: Telling Tulsa's Story 1
    Tulsa's Pentecostal Community 2
    The Tragedy and Triumph of Tulsa 3

Chapter 2: Pentecost in Oklahoma 7
    Pentecost in Lamont 8
    Pentecost in Doxey 10
    Black Pentecostals in Oklahoma 14
    Eastern Oklahoma 16

Chapter 3: Pentecost Comes to Tulsa 23
    The Town of Tallasi 23
    Early Pentecostal Revivals 24
    Pentecost in Greenwood 29
    North Greenwood Church of God in Christ 29
    5th and Peoria Mission 30
    Apostolic Faith State Encampment 33
    Mission of Redeeming Love 36
    Apostolic (Oneness) Church 37

Chapter 4: Pentecost in Green Country 39
    Bartlesville 39
    Bixby 41
    Broken Arrow 44
    Claremore 47
    Jenks/ 48
    Sand Springs 48
    Sapulpa 50
    Skiatook 51

Chapter 5: Tulsa's Race Massacre and the Pentecostal Survivors 53
    Tulsa's Forgotten History 53
    The Greenwood Community 54
    The Greenwood Massacre 55
    Pentecostal Survivors 58
    White Pentecostal Silence 68

Chapter 6: Revival in Greenwood 73
    North Greenwood-First Church of God in Christ 74
    Greater Lansing Church of God in Christ 76
    Historic Buford Colony 77

    New Bethel-South Haven 78
    Friendship Missionary Baptist Church 79

Chapter 7: Centennial Pentecostal Churches 81
    Aimee Semple McPherson 81
    Peoria and Haskell Mission/Woodlake 85
    Full Gospel Tabernacle 87
    Raymond T. Richey Revival 90
    Faith Tabernacle 93
    Pentecostal Rescue Mission 95
    Carbondale Assembly/West Tulsa Assembly 96
    1st Pentecostal Church/Metro Pentecostal Church 98

Chapter 8: Post-WWII Churches 101
    Greater Lansing Church of God in Christ 103
    First Church of God In Christ 104
    Northside Church of God in Christ 105
    Page Memorial Church of God in Christ 106
    Greater Grace & Pentecostal Assemblies of the World 108
    Mother Grace Tucker Ministries 110
    Church of the Silent Sheep 111
    Church of God 111
    Pentecostal Holiness Church/Evangelistic Temple 112
    Beams of Light and Grace Gospel Churches 116
    White Church in Broken Arrow 119
    Bethel Temple/New Life Center 120
    Sheridan Christian Center 122
    Church of God of Apostolic Faith 124
    Christian Chapel Assembly of God 126

Chapter 9: Tulsa's Healing Ministries 129
    Jack Coe 129
    Mildred Wicks 132
    Oral Roberts 134
    Oral Roberts University 138
    T. L. and Daisy Osborn 146
    Kenneth E. Hagin and Rhema Bible Church 148
    Carlton Pearson & Higher Dimensions 152

Chapter 10: Knowing the Past, Embracing the Future 157

Bibliography 163

Index 171

Preface

I have spent most of my life in Tulsa, Oklahoma. In 1985, my family moved to Bixby from Illinois when I was ten years old. Until that point, we had not lived in any one state more than three years. Thirty-five years later, this community has become my home with a significant anchor being my local Pentecostal church: Christian Chapel Assembly of God.

Although I grew up in a Methodist family, when I was saved shortly after high school, I ended up at an Assemblies of God church. I knew nothing about Pentecostalism, but the pastors mentored me and led me into receiving the baptism in the Holy Spirit. In a desire to find God's call on my life, I enrolled in Oral Roberts University (ORU) where I studied Church History.

My father was a history teacher early in his life. So growing up, I remember driving around to various historical sites to research our family history. That quest was deeply embedded in me. For my masters, I did research on the history of the Pentecostal and Charismatic Movement in ORU's Holy Spirit Research Center. The Director, Dr. Mark Roberts became a mentor and friend as I wrote my thesis on the life and theology of Howard M. Ervin, a founding faculty member. The HSRC helped me identify more fully with the tradition I had joined and gave me a love for the stories of its people. My Ph.D. research at Bangor University's Centre for Pentecostal Theology centered on the history of the Assemblies of God. Along the way, I found various bits of information about Tulsa and the surrounding areas, including two churches I had served: Christian Chapel in Tulsa and New Life Center in Broken Arrow.

In 2013, as the 100th Anniversary of the Oklahoma Assemblies of God was approaching the Lord placed it on my heart to write about the history of Pentecostal churches in Tulsa. However, at the time I was pastoring in Broken Arrow and did not have enough emotional energy to complete the project. After I completed my Ph.D. in 2017, Dr. Roberts, became the newly appointed dean of the ORU library and hired me to be the new director of the Holy Spirit Research Center. In this dream appointment, I have access to rich historical treasures, yet I soon noticed there was little resources on local Tulsa Spirit-filled churches. Considering my prior interest, collecting artifacts on Tulsa churches became a priority. This interest not only re-ignited my desire to collect Tulsa's history, but to tell the story as I had wanted to years before.

While working on an article about Oral Roberts' legacy of racial reconciliation, I became familiar with the story of Tulsa's 1921 Race Massacre and became curious about the fate of Tulsa's Black Pentecostal churches. I wondered why no one had questioned what happened to those churches. I knew that if I was going to tell the Pentecostal story, I had to include stories of black people and these churches. Even though I grew up in the city, the North Tulsa black community was unfamiliar to me. In years living in Tulsa, I had rarely set foot into its primarily black residential areas. I came to realize that my upbringing in the predominantly white South Tulsa suburban community had instilled attitudes and stereotypes about the black community as a place to be feared.

When I read about the Massacre, I realized why those attitudes were embedded in me. I had grown up with the same racially superior attitudes and stereotypes that led to the tragedy of 1921. Along the way I have grieved at my city's history and how the church was oblivious to the lives of black Christian believers. The first time I walked along the streets of the Greenwood neighborhood of Tulsa was less than two years ago. As a supposed "expert" on Pentecostalism, I knew little about this significant segment of Pentecostalism in my own home town.

In my world ignorance of people of color has been the norm. Confronting this norm has motivated me to bring the story of Tulsa's black Pentecostal Church in to the forefront. While white stories are also important, but many of them have been documented many times over. While those of our community's Black Pentecostals have been neglected for over 100 years. In part, this book seeks to uncover those stories and re-introduce black and white Pentecostals to each other as a tool to begin to heal our city of a broken racial past.

Daniel Isgrigg
March 2021

1

INTRODUCTION: TELLING TULSA'S STORY

Pentecostalism is over a century old. Beginning as an offshoot of the nineteenth-century Holiness Movement, it has become one of the fastest growing religious movements in the world. Its beginnings are traced to pockets of revival around the world at the turn of the twentieth century. In America, Pentecostalism traces its roots back to Charles Parham's Bible school in Topeka, Kansas where in 1901 students began to speak in tongues as the result of receiving the baptism in the Holy Spirit. But it was the Azusa Street Revival in Los Angeles, California in 1906 that ignited a fire that would spread Pentecost around the globe. Led by William J. Seymour, the son of emancipated slaves, the revival was ground zero for a global movement that today numbers 124 million adherents in classical Pentecostal denominations such as Church of God in Christ (COGIC), Pentecostal Holiness Church (IPHC), Church of God, Cleveland, TN (COG), Assemblies of God (AG), and the International Church of the Foursquare Gospel (ICFG).[1]

With its extraordinary beginnings among the poor and marginalized in American society, the Pentecostal story has received increased attention because Pentecostal history texts have acquainted the larger Christian community with its remarkable story. Among the growth of Pentecostal histories has been a number of biographies of early Pentecostal leaders who shaped the movement,

---

[1] See Todd Johnson and Gina Zurlo, *Introducing Spirit-empowered Christianity* (Tulsa, OK: ORU Press, 2020). Classical Pentecostals are generally recognized as a subset of the Holiness-evangelical tradition, identified by their distinctive beliefs in an experience subsequent to salvation called the baptism in the Holy Spirit accompanied by speaking in tongues and the exercise of the gifts of the Spirit.

including Seymour, J. H. King, C. H. Mason, and A. J. Tomlinson.

However, Pentecostalism is about more than denominations or individuals; it is a story about places where people encountered God through the Holy Spirit. When you think of the movement, you think of a mansion called "Stone's Folly" in Topeka, Kansas; an old mission on Azusa Street in Los Angeles; a campground in Falcon, North Carolina; or a temple in Memphis, Tennessee. Each of these locations, where people had life-changing encounters with God, represents a unique aspect of the story that shaped the movement as a whole. They are also places where men and women stepped out in faith to plant churches and to start new ministries that shaped and propelled the movement forward.

Tulsa's Pentecostal Community

This work chronicles the stories of the revivals, churches, and ministries that established the Pentecostal Movement in Tulsa, Oklahoma and the surrounding communities. Situated in the heart of Green Country in the Northeastern part of "The Sooner State," Tulsa is a city of great beauty and prosperity. Historically a deeply religious community, it is often referred to as the "buckle of the Bible Belt." Within its strong Christian heritage, Tulsa has become particularly famous for the Pentecostal-Charismatic ministries that made it their home. Yet, the Pentecostal story goes back to the beginnings of the town itself when revivals were held and churches were established in the newly discovered oil-boom town. Before Oklahoma became a state, Pentecostals were preaching the full gospel of salvation, sanctification, baptism in the Holy Spirit, healing, and the soon coming King in its streets, in tents, and in its churches.

According to 2010 Census data, there are over 100 Pentecostal churches with members numbering nearly 20,000 out of a population of 650,000 in Tulsa County.[2] Added to that number is an even greater number of independent and non-denominational Charismatic churches. The largest Pentecostal body in Tulsa

---

[2] "Tulsa County 2010," ARDA: Association of Religion Data Archives, accessed November 8, 2020, https://www.thearda.com/rcms2010/rcms2010a.asp?U=40143&T=county&S=family&Y=2010. The story of the Charismatic ministries deserve a whole volume unto themselves. But they will be briefly mentioned in this book.

County is the Assemblies of God whose nearly 13,000 adherents in 48 churches represent half of the total number of Pentecostals. United Pentecostal Church International (UPCI) congregations are second with 17 churches. Black Pentecostal churches, primarily from the Church of God in Christ, reported over 1,000 adherents in 7 congregations. With these demographics, Assemblies of God churches play a prominent role in Tulsa's story, not because they are more important, but because AG congregations had more data upon which to draw. Since other denominations also struggled to establish works in Tulsa, including the International Church of the Foursquare; Church of God (Cleveland, TN); Pentecostal Assemblies of the World, Church of God of Prophecy; and to some degree Pentecostal Holiness churches, effort was made to include their stories. While every story of every church could not be included, the aim has been to paint a representative picture of the people, churches, and denominations that made up the fabric of the Spirit-filled community in Tulsa.

The Triumph and Tragedy of Tulsa

Tulsa's Pentecostal story is interwoven with the tremendous advantages and disadvantages of this city. For as the title suggests, Pentecostalism has been shaped by two crucial elements: the triumph of Pentecostal revivals and the tragedy of the 1921 Tulsa Race Massacre.[3] These two aspects have shaped the Pentecostal community, both positively and negatively.

This is a story of how Tulsa became one of the most important epicenters for Pentecostal and Charismatic Christianity in the United States. It is the story of famous figures such as Charles Parham, Aimee Semple McPherson, and Raymond T. Richey, whose revival meetings helped establish some of the city's most important churches. It is also a story of local pastors and evangelists who preached the gospel and started new churches, nurtured established congregations, and

---

[3] Historically known as the Tulsa Race Riot, this volume will mostly refer to the event of 1921 as the Tulsa Race Massacre as it is most commonly held by the community today. The prior use of the word "riot" has been recognized more recently as problematic as it has been used as a way of placing blame on the Black community for the destruction associated with that event. There may be times when the term "riot" will be used to draw historical connections, while at the same time giving full recognition to the severity of this event as a massacre of Black people in Tulsa.

introduced people to the Spirit-filled life. For over a century, the Pentecostal message has found a home in the community as some of its best-known Pentecostal and Charismatic evangelists launched worldwide ministries that have impacted millions.

Tulsa's Pentecostal story also recounts the horrific events of the Race Massacre, which is marking its centennial in 2021. During a two-day period, white mobs assaulted the all-black community of Tulsa's famous Greenwood District, north of downtown Tulsa. They killed hundreds of people and set thirty-five blocks of homes, businesses, and churches ablaze. While this book reveals the untold story of the resilient Black Pentecostal community that endured the racial violence and revived Greenwood, racial tensions still profoundly impact Tulsa's social and geographical realities to the point that most Tulsa Pentecostal churches are homogenous and geographically isolated.

Fifty years after one of the first Black Pentecostal scholars, James Tinney, asked, "Is it not strange that no one has inquired about the origin of Black Pentecostal bodies?"[4] We can ask that same question about Tulsa's Pentecostal history. For generations, white Tulsa ignored the story of the 1921 destruction of the Greenwood community. Until now, their general reluctance to discuss the incident and its ramifications has left the story of Tulsa's Black Pentecostal Church and its development unexpressed.

Because Black contribution has been so often neglected in American religious history, this story intentionally focuses on the experiences of Black Pentecostals and churches in Tulsa.[5] The lives and experiences of Black Pentecostal believers have value and deserve to be told. Yet the significance of Tulsa's African American community is noticeably absent from its Pentecostal histories. Considering that the largest body of Pentecostals in the U.S. is African American,

---

[4] Ithiel C. Clemmons, *Bishop Mason and the Roots of the Church of God in Christ* (Bakersfield, CA: Pneumalife Publishing, 1997), 37.

[5] This study draws in the insights of Ashton Crawley, *Blackpentecostal Breath: The Aesthetics of Possibility* (New York: Fordham University Press, 2017), who places reference to Black Pentecostalism as part of a wider field of Black Study, which recognizes the uniqueness of African American experiences even within a larger body like Pentecostalism (15).

in the Church of God in Christ, it is right to emphasize that the study of Pentecostalism without blackness is not a study of Pentecostalism at all.[6]

The privileges of money, education, and societal advantages made it possible for white denominations to publish, distribute, and archive materials. The scarcity of primary sources makes piecing together the story of the Black Pentecostal Church more difficult. Early minute books and periodical literature from Black Pentecostal groups are limited. Decades of racism and systemic poverty have resulted in a significant loss of institutional memory for these churches. One also has to wonder what materials there might have been to tell the story of the black church in Tulsa had they not burned with the rest of Greenwood. Nevertheless, with the help of several pastors and community leaders, the stories of Tulsa's Black Pentecostal Churches can, finally, be chronicled in print.[7]

My position of privilege as a white Pentecostal from south Tulsa challenges my ability to accurately contextualize the Black Pentecostal story. Navigating this challenge leads me to prioritize the Black Pentecostal story and let the community speak for itself. While admittedly, these attempts may fall short at points, I ask grace from the readers and hope that those who come after me will bring more light to this story.

The story of Tulsa's Pentecostal Church is one of growth and miracles. This book explores Tulsa's religious ethos and how it became a headquarters for Pentecostal and Charismatic Christianity. But it also attempts to right some of the wrongs that occurred within its boundaries by telling the story of Pentecostalism in Tulsa, documenting both the tragedies and triumphs of Spirit-filled people.

---

[6] See Estrelda Alexander, *Black Fire: One Hundred Years of African American Pentecostalism* (Downers Grove, IL: IVP Academic, 2011). Seymour Press has contributed significantly to the increase in published academic histories of Black Pentecostal denominations and individuals.

[7] Some of the best historical resources are interviews with individuals from local congregations. This has proved exceedingly difficult as this research was conducted primarily during the 2020 COVID-19. Added to this is the reality that many of the survivors have now passed away. However, I am grateful to Dr. Sherri Tapp, Pastor Brian Wilson, Bishop L. V. Broom, and James Goodwin who shared their knowledge and connected me with other important individuals during my research.

2

PENTECOST IN OKLAHOMA

Our story must begin with how the winds of revival reached Oklahoma. Prior to statehood in 1907, Oklahoma consisted of two territories: Indian Territory in the East and Oklahoma Territory in the West. Beginning in the 1880s, homesteaders from around the U. S. claimed 160-acre plots across Oklahoma that previously belonged to the Native American tribes. Among these "sooners" were Holiness groups who came to establish Holiness communities and preach their revivalist message. The most significant among these was the Fire-Baptized Holiness Church founded by Benjamin Hardin Irwin, a revivalist who preached salvation, a "second blessing" sanctification (which he called baptism in the Holy Ghost) and a third experience he called the "baptism of fire."[1] Although he didn't normalize speaking in tongues, it was sometimes manifested in his meetings among other experiences such as "falling under the power." Irwin's three-stage experiences anchored in the Holy Spirit set the stage for the Holiness-Pentecostal Movement. As Vinson Synan notes, "In the social, doctrinal and intellectual sense, the Fire-Baptized Holiness Church was a direct precursor of the modern Pentecostal movement."[2]

In 1897, Irwin had preached his "baptism of fire" throughout Central Oklahoma, including Oklahoma City and El Reno.[3] It was no surprise, then, that Pentecost would break out in Oklahoma following the revival at the Azusa Street Mission in 1906 as many holiness believers caught the Pentecostal fire that was falling. In Oklahoma, Pentecostal fires were moving from two directions: Lamont

---

[1] Vinson Synan, *The Holiness-Pentecostal Movement in the United States* (Grand Rapids, MI: Eerdmans Publishing, 1971), 61-66.

[2] ibid., 68.

[3] "Brother Irwin's Letter," *The Way of Faith*, October 20, 1897, 2.

and Doxey in the West and Tahlequah and Muskogee in the East. These fires would eventually converge in Tulsa. We begin with that story.

Pentecost in Lamont

Nestled in the tall grass prairies just north of Enid in Central Oklahoma is the tiny town of Lamont. Around the turn of the twentieth century, Lamont became the location for the Fire-Baptized Holiness Association of Oklahoma. In 1902, the FBHA disbanded, but many in the area continued to pursue a Pentecostal experience. In 1905, in the nearby town of Billings, holiness preacher, Harry P. Lott, held a revival meeting in which a couple who were seeking the fire-baptized experience began to speak in tongues.[4] Lott was unfamiliar with that experience at the time, but established a holiness church there and word spread around the area of this new experience.

In December 1906, Glenn A. Cook came from the Azusa Street Mission to hold meetings in Lamont. Cook had come to the Azusa Revival as a skeptic intent on correcting Seymour's preaching about the Holy Spirit.[5] But after he witnessed the power of God in the meetings, he accepted the Pentecostal message and became an early leader in the mission. In December 1906, Cook set off to Chicago on the Rock Island Railway. On his way, he stopped in Lamont where he visited a group of Fire-Baptized Holiness believers who were hungry for the Pentecostal experience. However, he recognized that some of their Holiness traditions, such as abstaining from coffee and neckties, were hindrances to receiving the baptism in the Holy Spirit. Cook testified that, "after about ten days of prayer and holding up the blood, God began to break them up and they began to beg pardon of one another." It wasn't long before God poured out his Spirit and people came from 100 miles away to "get Pentecost and healing."[6] After two weeks leading the revival, Cook left for Chicago.

---

[4] Joseph E. Campbell, *The Pentecostal Holiness Church: Its History and Its Background* (Eugene, OR: Wipf & Stock, 2016), 208-209.

[5] Cecil M. Robeck, Jr., *The Azusa Street Mission and Revival: The Birth of the Global Movement* (Nashville: Nelson Reference & Electronic, 2006), 91-93.

[6] G. A. Cook, "Pentecost in Lamont," *Apostolic Faith,* January 1907, 1.

In May of 1907, J. H. King was invited to join Cook at Lamont for another Fire-Baptized Holiness revival.[7] He had received the baptism in the Holy Spirit a few months earlier and was instrumental in reviving the Fire-Baptized Holiness Church after Irwin departed. King reluctantly accepted the invitation, as he was already engaged in a revival in Valdosta, Alabama. And though King did not know Cook, he had heard good things about him. However, when King arrived, Cook shared his objection to sanctification as a definite experience.[8] He was deeply disturbed that the Pentecostal work at Lamont was "wrecked and ruined" by Cook's lax view of holiness.[9] After Cook left the meeting, King took over, re-emphasizing the doctrine of holiness and sanctification as a prerequisite for receiving the baptism in the Holy Spirit.

In July 1907, G. B. Cashwell of Dunn, North Carolina came to the city to hold a two-week campmeeting.[10] Mrs. R. M. Ellis of nearby Billings, who was filled with the Spirit in Lamont, testified that her husband was baptized in the Holy Ghost, proclaiming, "I never heard such doctrine preached before."[11] In May 1908, Harry P. Lott came to hold a three-week campmeeting. With him was A. S. Copley of Kansas City, Missouri.[12] King, Cashwell, and Lott helped stabilize the revival in Lamont and make it the place to be to experience Pentecost.

From Lamont, small revivals were springing up in many communities in North Central Oklahoma. In January 1907, Arthur E. Grimshaw held a meeting in Pawhuska about which he writes, "We have Pentecost here and its glorious!" But Grimshaw was particularly impressed that Pentecost could fall even "among the cowboys and farmers in this country."[13] Mrs. J. Y. Clark, received Pentecost in Lamont then started a revival in the nearby town of Billings.[14] She excitedly

---

[7] Vinson Synan, *Old Time Power: A Centennial History of the Pentecostal Holiness Church* (Franklin Springs, GA: LifeSprings, 1998), 116.

[8] J. H. King, *Yet Speaketh* (Franklin Springs, GA: The Publishing House of the Pentecostal Holiness Church, 1949), 127.

[9] King, *Yet Speaketh*, 127. King was particularly offended by statements by Cook about his tolerance for saloons and the sale of whiskey.

[10] "Local News," *Billings News*, May 17, 1907, 4; *Apostolic Faith*, May 1907, 2.

[11] "Billings, Oklahoma," *Bridegroom's Messenger*, February 1, 1908, 3. Regarding the use of "Mrs.," many Pentecostal papers used the name of the husband rather than their own first name.

[12] "Pentecostal Camp Meetings," *Bridegroom's Messenger*, April 15, 1908, 2.

[13] *Apostolic Faith*, January 1907, 4.

[14] "Billings, Okla.," *Bridegroom's Messenger*, May 1, 1908, 2.

reports in the *Bridegroom's Messenger*, "Two received their Pentecost and ten were converted, among whom were my son and his wife. Oh glory!"[15] In May 1910, the revival fires were burning in nearby Tonkawa, east of Billings, in the tents of Lott, R. B. Beall and King.[16]

But the revivals in and around Lamont were often hard to sustain without the presence of these major early Pentecostal leaders. By 1912, as the fires in Lamont were beginning to cool, Brother F. E. Short reported there was "not much encouragement" when he arrived to conduct his meeting there.[17] Despite the waning revival in the area, a significant revival was held in 1914 in Blackwell by Sadie (Phillips) Kelly, who preached the Oneness message of baptism in Jesus's name under a brush arbor. According to United Pentecostal Church (UPCI) history, Kelly was the niece of Frank Phillips, the wealthy founder of Phillips Petroleum in Bartlesville. Her children and grandchildren continued in ministry with the UPCI for several years after her death.[18]

This small town of Lamont was the important catalyst for seven years of revival fires (1907-1914) in the surrounding communities. What began here would establish the Pentecostal movement throughout Oklahoma.

Pentecost in Doxey

Several Fire-Baptized Holiness communities sprang up in Carter County, in Western Oklahoma Territory. Calvary Creek Mission in Cordell was established in 1900 and more importantly the Beulah Home in Doxey was established near Sayre in 1906.[19] The mission at Doxey was established by a group called the "Indian Creek Band."[20] The story begins in 1896 when a teenaged Jerry Osborn was practicing preaching on Acts chapter 2 in a cave in the Hill Creek community of Texas. On his way home, Osborn stopped along the road to pray and suddenly was

---

[15] "Billings, Okla.," *Bridegroom's Messenger*, March 1, 1908, 2.
[16] "A Pentecostal Campmeeting," *Apostolic Evangel*, April 1, 1910, 2.
[17] "Letter from Brother Short," *Apostolic Evangel*, February 1, 1912, 3.
[18] Garrison and Westberg, *Claiming the Land*, 20.
[19] "E. D. Wells Letter," *Live Coals of Fire*, January 26, 1900, 6.
[20] Campbell, *The Pentecostal Holiness Church: Its History and Its Background*, 508-509.

filled with the Holy Spirit. He began speaking in tongues and started laughing and shouting for joy.[21] Excited by his experience, Osborn shared the message of the baptism in the Spirit to all of his neighbors.

Shortly after his powerful experience, Osborn met Frank T. Alexander who lived on Chalk Mountain near Glen Rose, Texas. Alexander moved to Oklahoma to claim a homestead in the newly settled territory near Carter. Once settled, Alexander invited Osborn to help start a church in Carter among the new settlers and cowboys who came through the area.[22] One of the first to receive the baptism was a Native American woman who, according Osborn, knew only two words of English, but when the Spirit came on her she began to speak in tongues. During another meeting, some cowboys came in to mock the service. By the end, one cowboy came to the altar, but he didn't know how to pray. Osborn told him to just talk to God as he does the cowboys. The cowboy lifted his hands and prayed, "Ole, Buddy, Ole, Pal. If you got something for me, just slip it to me right now!"[23]

A few years later, Alexander built the two-story Beulah home that also housed an orphanage and Immanuel Bible school.[24] Joining him was Osborn, William Stale, F. D. Hare, and R. E. Winsett. Despite Alexander's friendship with Osborn, he had not yet received the baptism in the Spirit. So, in May 1907, Alexander traveled to Lamont with several of the Beulah residents to a campmeeting led by King and G. B. Cashwell. Alexander had a powerful experience of "lying under the power" for hours and spoke in tongues.[25] Alexander brought the experience back with him to the Beulah Home and by August 1908, Alexander was holding his own campmeetings."[26]

News of the revival was regularly featured on the front page of the Pentecostal newspaper, *The Bridegroom's Messenger*. R. E. Winsett proclaimed, "this is an apostolic town."[27] Doxey quickly became a center for Pentecostal revival fires in that area

---

[21] Betty Treece, *Come to Beulah Land: The Pioneer Preacher Jerry Earl Osborn 1879-1964* (Lake Charles, LA: n.p., 1997), 67–68.

[22] Jack C. Garrison and Barbara Westberg, *Claiming the Land: A History of the United Pentecostal Church in the Great State of Oklahoma* (Oklahoma District United Pentecostal Church, 2012), 17.

[23] Treece, *Come to Beulah Land*, 92.

[24] R. E. Winsett, "Beulah Home," *Bridegroom's Messenger*, November 15, 1908, 2.

[25] "Billings, Okla.," *Bridegroom's Messenger*, March 1, 1908, 2; Campbell, *The Pentecostal Holiness Church*, 211.

[26] Frank T. Alexander, "Apostolic Camp Meeting," *Bridegroom's Messenger*, July 14, 1908, 2.

[27] Winsett, "Beulah Home," 2.

and several important evangelists visited the revival. In 1909, Fire-Baptized Holiness leader, F. M. Britton of Falcon North Carolina led at least ten Holiness preachers into the baptism of the Holy Spirit and speaking in tongues.[28] Britton rejoiced at the influence this mission was having on Holiness believers in Texas and Oklahoma. Another notable preacher at this campmeeting meeting was former Baptist pastor, E. N. Bell from Fort Worth, Texas, who would become an early Assemblies of God leader. Dan and Dolly York, important Pentecostal Holiness evangelists who helped establish IPHC works in the South, also received the Holy Spirit in Doxey.[29] A. B. Cox, another attendee was an important early Assemblies of God leader, who led J. W. Welch into the Pentecostal experience in Eastern Oklahoma.[30]

2.1 Beulah Home at Doxey (IFPHC)

Among the well-known teachers at the Bible school was Daniel Awrey, a notable early Pentecostal evangelist, Bible teacher, and missionary. Awrey received the baptism in the Holy Spirit in December 1890 in the Christian Missionary Alliance Bible School in Alliance, Ohio. [31] His testimony of a pre-1900 Spirit baptism made him legendary in Pentecostal circles. Hearing of Alexander's new

---

[28] F. M. Britton, "Camp Meeting Notes," *Bridegroom's Messenger,* October 1, 1909, 1

[29] Campbell, *The Pentecostal Holiness Church,* 211.

[30] Glenn Gohr, "A. B. and Dora Cox," *Assemblies of God Heritage* (Summer 1995): 9-11, 31.

[31] Daniel Awrey, "Life Sketches," *The Latter Rain Evangel,* March 1910, 19-23.

school, Awrey made his way to Doxey to teach there from 1908-1909.[32] Another teacher, R. E. Winsett, taught music and published the first Pentecostal hymnbook, *Songs of Pentecostal Power*.[33] Winsett later moved to Hot Springs, Arkansas and then Cleveland, Tennessee. His hymnbooks became the standard for early Pentecostals. The presence of Awrey and Winsett greatly boosted the revival. Awrey sent students from the School to surrounding towns such as Sayer and Carter. One of the attendees of the meetings testified, "After months of seeking... I received the Holy Ghost with Bible evidence of speaking in tongues. This was July 5, 1909, on my fiftieth birthday, and I never felt younger in my life."[34]

In 1905, around the same time as the revivals in Lamont and Doxey, several women were praying for a Pentecostal revival in Oklahoma City. In January 1906, R. B. Beall, Oscar C. Wilkins, and Lott opened a Fire-Baptized Holiness-Pentecostal work in the Blue Front Saloon downtown.[35] A few months later, Lott received the baptism in the Holy Spirit and spoke in tongues on August 24, 1907.[36] He became an important leader who established Pentecostal Holiness churches across Oklahoma, including Billings, Pawnee, Muskogee, McAllister, Stratford, Yukon and Paul's Valley.[37]

Dan T. Muse, a notable, much beloved minister came out of the IPHC work in Oklahoma City. Muse served as Oklahoma Conference Superintendent and eventually Bishop of the Pentecostal Holiness Church (1937–1950).[38]

---

[32] Al Warner, "Daniel Awrey: Azusa Street Itinerant Missionary Evangelist" (paper presented at the 44th Annual Meeting of the Society for Pentecostal Studies, Southeastern University, Lakeland, FL, March 13, 2015), 10.

[33] "Pentecostal Songbooks," *Bridegroom's Messenger*, November 1, 1908, 2.

[34] "My Testimony," *Bridegroom's Messenger*, March 15, 1910, 2.

[35] Campbell, *The Pentecostal Holiness Church*, 210.

[36] "The Work in Oklahoma City," August 1, 1908, 1.

[37] Campbell, *The Pentecostal Holiness Church*, 211.

[38] Harold Paul, *Dan T. Muse: From Printer's Devil to Bishop* (Franklin Springs, GA: Advocate Press, 1976).

Black Pentecostals in Oklahoma

After the Civil War, Oklahoma became an important haven for African Americans in the South. Many families moved to Oklahoma and established all–black towns in hopes of a new life apart from the Jim Crow South.[39] As the territories welcomed African American families, churches quickly followed. Important to the Tulsa story is the arrival in Oklahoma of the Church of God in Christ (COGIC), the historically Black Holiness-Pentecostal denomination founded by Charles H. Mason and C. P. Jones in 1895. Originally a Holiness Baptist minister, Mason accepted the Pentecostal message and in 1906 went to the Azusa Mission to experience the baptism in the Spirit for himself. His new understanding of the Holy Spirit caused a split with Jones in which Mason left to lead the COGIC church as a distinctly Pentecostal denomination. Mason's early influence was primarily in the South, including Oklahoma.

There are few details about the earliest COGIC congregations in Oklahoma. But, the 1907 Convocation listed at least two congregations in Oklahoma.[40] With the number of congregations growing over the next few years, in 1912, Mason sent Bishop O. T. Jones and his brother, Bishop Arthur Jones, to set churches in order.[41] When Jones arrived in Enid, he met a young Baptist minister named John Morris who established the first Pentecostal work near Enid in 1910.[42] His twin daughters, Reatha and Leatha, known as the "The Twins" became early church planters in the Church of God in Christ.[43]

Recognizing the calling on Reatha and Leatha, Mother Lizzie Robinson commissioned them as evangelists. As Anthea Butler has documented, Robinson

---

[39] Hannibal B. Johnson, *Acres of Aspiration: The All-black Towns in Oklahoma* (Austin, TX: Eakin Press, 2002).

[40] Clemmons, *Bishop Mason and the Roots of the Church of God in Christ*, 66. See also, *Census of Religious Bodies 1926, Church of God in Christ*, 9, Department of Commerce, United States of America (Washington, DC: Government Printing Office, 1929).

[41] Clemmons, *Bishop Mason and the Roots of the Church of God in Christ*, 84; Bobby Bean, *This is the Church of God in Christ* (Atlanta: Underground Epics Pub., 2001), 175.

[42] Glenda Williams Goodson, "The Church of God in Christ Transforms Women's Ministries through the Positive Influence of the Chief Apostle Bishop C. H. Mason," in *With Signs Following: The Life and Ministry of Charles Harrison Mason*, ed. Raynard D. Smith (St. Louis: Christian Board of Publication, 2015), 92.

[43] Doris J. Sims, *Roots Out of Dry Ground: The Mother Reatha Herndon Story* (Brooklyn, NY: Welstar Publishing, 2014), 1.

and her team of church mothers were largely responsible for early COGIC church planting efforts, including in Oklahoma.[44] The sisters' first crusade was held in Nowata, alongside O. T. Jones.[45] Mother Reatha Herndon recalls,

> We'd put them on that Mourner's Bench and then we'd get over those people, casting out devils, praying for them and blessing them.... Sometime in the meetings there would be 15 and 20 people who would get saved. Most of them would be filled with the Holy Ghost.[46]

Over her ministry career, God used Mother Reatha to establish seventy-five churches around the United States and she is recognized as one of the greatest church planters in the early Church of God in Christ.

The person most responsible for establishing black Pentecostal churches in Oklahoma, however, was Bishop E. M. Page, one of the original Elders of the Church of God in Christ. Page served as the State Overseer for Oklahoma from 1917–1926 and was responsible for growing the number of churches in his jurisdiction from twelve to over 100 across Oklahoma and Texas. He founded the COGIC work in Muskogee and Oklahoma City, where he established the denomination's Oklahoma headquarters.[47] By 1926, there were 59 churches in the state (the fourth highest number in the U.S. behind Texas, Mississippi, and Arkansas), 48 buildings, 1,700 members.[48] Today, Page Sanctuary Church of God in Christ in Oklahoma City, which he founded in 1929, serves as a memorial to his work.[49]

2.2 E. M. Page c. 1920

---

[44] Anthea D. Butler, *Women in the Church of God in Christ: Making a Sanctified World* (Chapel Hill: University of North Carolina Press, 2007), 50.

[45] Sims,, *Roots Out of Dry Ground*, 82, refers to it as "Newwater," but that is likely mistaken for Nowata, where an established church is said to be connected to O. T. Jones' work in the town.

[46] ibid., 89.

[47] *Yearbook of the Church of God in Christ* (Memphis, TN: Church of God in Christ, 1926), 66-67.

[48] *Census of Religious Bodies 1926, Church of God in Christ*, 7-8.

[49] "History of the Page Sanctuary Church of God in Christ," accessed July 7, 2020, http://www.pagesanctuarycogic.org/church-history.php.

Eastern Oklahoma

As Pentecost was moving in Western Oklahoma, another fire was spreading in Northeastern part of the territories. With its close proximity to Parham's revivals in Galena, Kansas, word spread about Pentecost into the area as early as 1903. Parham's 1904 Joplin revival drew believers from Miami, Oklahoma.[50] In 1909, an Apostolic Faith preacher used his horse and wagon to travel down the Grand River toward Tahlequah and reported "seven saved, seven sanctified and one baptized in the Holy Ghost."[51] In 1910, Edward M. Pearson came to Welch, Oklahoma and preached the Apostolic Faith. One convert was Frank Yadon, whom Pearson told about Pentecost when he stayed in their home.[52]

From Miami, Pentecost moved south to the tribal towns of Muskogee and Tahlequah. These two towns in the heart of Indian Territory eventually became significant centers for Pentecostalism in Eastern Oklahoma. Muskogee served as the seat of the Union Agency for the Five Civilized Tribes in 1875 and the capital of Indian Territory. Tahlequah was established as the home of the Cherokee people in 1839 when they were forced to come to Indian Territory on the Trail of Tears.

Muskogee

In 1910, John W. Welch was leading a Christian Missionary Alliance missionary in Muskogee. He knew there was more to the Holy Spirit than just sanctification.[53] In 1912, Welch heard about the Pentecostal experience in a campmeeting led by A. B. Cox and was filled with the Holy Spirit several months later.[54] The members of

---

[50] Klaude Kendrick, *The Promise Fulfilled: A History of the Pentecostal Movement* (Springfield, MO: 1959), 60.

[51] "Extracts from Precious Letters," *Apostolic Faith* (Portland), April 1909, 2.

[52] Garrison and Westberg, *Claiming the Land*, 20. See also, Grace Yadon Wiens, *Unto You and to Your Children: The Yandon Family Story* (Hazelwood, MO: Word Aflame Press, 2004).

[53] Carl Brumback, *Suddenly ... From Heaven: A History of the Assemblies of God* (Springfield, MO: Gospel Publishing House, 1961), 166.

[54] A. B. Cox, "Siloam Springs," *Bridegroom's Messenger*, February 1, 1912, 3; Also, Burke, *Like a Prairie Fire*, 30-31.

the Welch's Alliance mission rejected his new teaching on speaking in tongues and quickly abandoned him, whereupon he re-opened his church as the first Pentecostal mission in Muskogee.

The town was also an important early center for COGIC Churches. In 1917, Page moved from Arkansas to Muskogee to establish a church.[55] As overseer of Oklahoma, he was instrumental in planting several other churches, including an early church in Sapulpa. Another COGIC bishop, William Elijah Jefferies was born in Leota, Kansas, but his family moved to Muskogee. He was saved, sanctified, and filled with the Holy Ghost in Murphy, Oklahoma. He served with Page and Bishop Travis B. Sipuel as state president of the Youth Department and, later, as State Bishop.[56] By 1925, COGIC churches could be found throughout Eastern Oklahoma including Muskogee, Okmulgee, McAlister, Eufaula, Okay, Henryetta, Vian, Antlers, Sawyer, and Idabel.[57]

A strong Oneness Pentecostal presence was established west of Muskogee, in the small town of Dewar, near Henryetta. Dewar is one of the oldest Oneness Pentecostal churches in Oklahoma. Beginning in 1905, Howard Goss had visited the town following his meetings in Tahlequah.[58] Sometime in 1912, the first church building called "The Little Green Mission"[59] was organized with the Pentecostal Assemblies of the World while it was a Trinitarian organization. In 1917, S. C. McClain traveled to Dewar where he found these Pentecostal believers. He preached the Oneness message with great success and baptized the whole church in "Jesus Name."[60]

Two years later, evangelist James Duca held a revival in the city, reporting that, "[w]e are having the grandest meeting… that I ever saw. Every time we meet

---

[55] *Yearbook of the Church of God in Christ (1926)*, 66-67.

[56] *The 41st Annual Convocation: Church of God in Christ* (Memphis, TN: Church of God in Christ, 1948), 23, Pentecostal and Charismatic Research Archive, accessed December 21, 2020, http://digitallibrary.usc.edu/cdm/compoundobject/collection/p15799coll14/id/245201/rec/9.

[57] *Yearbook of the Church of God in Christ (1926)*, 100-102.

[58] Don Martin, *The First Pentecostal Church of Garden City/ First Pentecostal Church of Tulsa Story* (Tulsa, OK: Don Martin, 2003), 12.

[59] "Mining Was Reason for Dewar's Being," *Daily Free Lance*, July 16, 1939, n.p.

[60] S. D. McClain and Robin Johnson, *Seek First the Kingdom* (Hazelwood, MO: Word Aflame Press, 2005), 54.

together [the Spirit] begins to rain down and as we continue services it gets harder and harder."[61]

2.3 Dewar PAW Church - 1917 (Don Martin)

To the west in the larger town of Spelter City, F. W. Pryor and G. C. Jones were holding cottage meetings. Pryor notes that at least thirty people were filled with the Holy Ghost. Jones preached the meetings, and many were baptized in Jesus's name. In nearby Henryetta, the Apostolic Church was founded in 1919 by John Renison.[62] In Morris, the first Pentecostal church, established in 1911, became Oneness in 1922 when Theodore Smith baptized many of the believers in "Jesus Name."[63]

Tahlequah

The first mention of Pentecost in Indian Territory is when Howard Goss came to Tahlequah in 1905. That year, Goss had received the baptism in the Holy Spirit in Galena, Kansas, and was invited by S. D. Kinne to preach the Apostolic Faith message at a revival. Goss experienced first-hand the dramatic Oklahoma

---

[61] "Dewar, Okla.," *The Blessed Truth*, January 15, 1919, 4.
[62] Garrison and Westberg, *Claiming the Land*, 184.
[63] Martin, *The First Pentecostal Church of Garden City/ First Pentecostal Church of Tulsa Story*, 12.

weather. His afternoon meeting started at over 90 degrees, but by its end that evening, attendees were trapped in an ice storm.[64]

In 1910, W. T. Gaston was invited by Vache A. Hargis to pastor the Pentecostal church in Tahlequah. The Tahlequah Assembly held services in various storefronts in the winter and in an open-air tabernacle in the summers. Eventually a small church was built at 300 N. Maple as a more permanent location, where it remained for many years.[65] When Gaston left for Tulsa in 1912, several notable evangelists visited Tahlequah to fill in and preach, including Willard H. Pope, A. B. Cox, and M. M. Pinson.[66]

Vache A. Hargis and his family had been saved in one of the early revivals.[67] He served as an evangelist and the interim pastor when the pastorate was open. His reputation earned him the respect to be elected first Secretary of the Oklahoma District of the Assemblies of God in 1914.

Other notable converts of Gaston's Tahlequah ministry include W. H. Boyles, a Cherokee, and Anderson Cathey, the "Pioneer of Pentecost" to Tahlequah's Native American community. In 1915, Boyles held a meeting for Cherokees in the town and over 500 people attended per night.[68]

This informal group of ministers held William Durham's "Finished Work" understanding of sanctification. They rejected the Wesleyan Holiness view of a three works of grace and accepted only two works: salvation and baptism in the Holy Spirit. Several in the group joined E. N. Bell, Howard Goss, and D. C. O. Opperman to conduct meetings under the name of the Apostolic Faith or Pentecostal but distanced themselves from the controversial Charles Parham.[69] Seeking to establish credentials for their loose association, in 1912, Goss arranged for C. H. Mason to provide credentials under the umbrella of the

---

[64] Ethel Goss, *Winds of God* (New York: Comet Press Books, 1958), 157. Garrison and Westberg, *Claiming the Land*, 19.

[65] Leroy Wesley Hawkins, "A History of the Assemblies of God in Oklahoma: The Formative Years, 1914–1929" (B. A. Thesis, Panhandle State College, Goodwell, Oklahoma, 1964), 35, 57.

[66] "Tahlequah," *Word and Witness*, December 20, 1913, 3.

[67] Burke, *Like a Prairie Fire*, 30-31.

[68] Hawkins, "A History of the Assemblies of God in Oklahoma," 36.

[69] Bell, "Notice About Parham," *Word and Witness*, October 1910, 3.

Church of God in Christ. Included in this group were Gaston and Welch.[70]

Another group of Holiness-Pentecostals, The Church of God of Apostolic Faith (COGAF), continued the original teachings of Parham.[71] They began when Edwin A. Buckles was saved in March 1909 and a few months later received sanctification. In July 1909, he was pastoring a Methodist church in Cedarville, Arkansas. When a party of Pentecostal evangelists came to town a few months later, he attended their meeting to fight against their teaching. Instead, he was convinced and received his own Holy Spirit baptism. In 1914, in response to the forming of the Assemblies of God, Buckles established a Holiness-Pentecostal fellowship called the Church of God of Apostolic Faith at the first General Conference held in Ozark, Arkansas.

Meanwhile, around the same time in the small town of Hulbert, west of Tahlequah, Mr. and Mrs. T. W. Capps had recently accepted the full gospel message through connections to Apostolic Faith believers in Kansas. Capps, who was from Tahlequah, came to Hulbert to hold a revival.[72] His daughter, Georgia Capps, had just married Oscar H. Bond. He was a non-believer who suffered from a nervous breakdown and an addiction to opioids. During Capps' revival, Bond began to soften to the gospel message. On January 1915, Capps invited Bond to accompany him to a revival at the Wagoner Pentecostal Holiness Church, where Brother Beal was the pastor.[73] Night after night Bond went to the altar until he "prayed straight through" to the baptism in the Holy Spirit. During the final week of the Wagoner revival, Edwin Buckles preached and baptized Bond in water.[74]

Bond and his wife joined the ministry and preached the Holiness-Pentecostal faith in revivals across Eastern Oklahoma, regularly traveling to Tulsa, Drumright and around Tahlequah. He was elected secretary of COGAF in 1916 and

---

[70] "Ordained Ministers in the Churches of God in Christ with their Locations Aug 1, 1912," Flower Pentecostal Heritage Center, August 1, 1912. See *Word and Witness*, December 20, 1913, 4. Oklahomans on this list include these include John and Myrtle Corbell of Ardmore, A. B. Cox of Doxey who had moved to Arkansas, F. D. Hall of Carter, Fred and Elva Marsh of Oklahoma City, Willard Pope of Tulsa, and Fayette Romines of Shawnee

[71] Adapted from "History of COGAF," The Church of God of the Apostolic Faith, accessed December 15, 2020, https://www.cogaf.org/what-we-do.

[72] O. H. Bond, *Life Story of O. H. Bond* (Oakgrove, AR: n.p., n.d.), 30.

[73] Bond, *Life Story of O. H. Bond*, 31.

[74] ibid., 42.

published the paper, *The Apostolic Faith Messenger*. COGAF established a campground in Stilwell, Oklahoma, near Tahlequah for their annual meetings. In 1955, the COGAF headquarters was established in Tulsa.

Another important COGAF revival was held near Ramona the "Happy Hill" church established in 1916 in the Ringo Schoolhouse. Holiness revivalists often visited the area and preached the Pentecostal blessing. In 1921, the Ringo school board kicked the church out, and they moved into a barn owned by John and Martha Street. They named it the Street Mission, until a decade later when it joined the COGAF. The name "Happy Hill" was given because the people were known for laughing, shouting, and crying in the Spirit. Today, it is the flagship church of the COGAF national office.[75]

---

[75] Adapted from the history of Happy Hill Church: "Our Story," Happy Hill, accessed November 17, 2020, https://www.happyhill.org/history.

3

PENTECOST COMES TO TULSA

The Town of Tallasi

In its earliest days as an Indian Territory, Tulsa was the home of the Creek Council Oak Tree that marked the end of the Trail of Tears prior to Oklahoma's Statehood. Forcefully removed by American expansion, members of the Muskogee Creek Nation were relocated near the Arkansas River in a place they later named *Tallasi* or Tulsa. Having adopted European values, some of the tribes owned black slaves, who were emancipated as "freedmen" following the Civil War and stayed in the area.

Because of the opportunity for freedmen settlements, African Americans from other parts of the South migrated to Oklahoma to establish all-black towns where they could be free from the growing tide of lynching and other injustices.[1] But that vision was short lived as the government also opened the lands to white settlers.

When oil was discovered in 1905 at the Glenn Pool, oilmen and companies came from all over to get in on the prosperity. New businesses and buildings were added to the once cow town. In 1907, the area was becoming an oil boomtown and Oklahoma applied for statehood. Despite the state's diversity, white settlers in Oklahoma were anything but tolerant of Native or African Americans. As the white population increased, blacks were forced to form their own "all blacktown within a town."[2] Shortly after receiving Statehood, Oklahoma went from a haven of racial diversity to one of the most segregated states in the Union. The

---

[1] James S. Hirsch, *Riot and Remembrance* (Boston: Houghton Mifflin, 2002), 34-35.
[2] Johnson, *Acres of Aspiration*, 169.

Constitutional Convention, led by the racial extremist president, William H. Murray, was determined to "out-Jim Crow the other southern states."[3] New laws ensured that black Tulsans would be separated from white Tulsans, unless serving as domestic or service workers in the developing affluent city.

Yet, Tulsa's new economic opportunities benefited white and black citizens. Its population exploded from 1,390 in 1900 to 18,000 in 1910; of these, an estimated 10,000 were African American.[4] Although Jim Crow laws resulted in a separate all-black community outside city limits, segregation became an opportunity for African Americans to reinvest in Greenwood—their own economic district—where entrepreneurs built churches, banks, hotels, entertainment establishments, and other businesses. By 1920, the Greenwood District—later known as Tulsa's Black Wallstreet—was one of the most successful black commercial districts in the country.[5] Alongside the growing economic center, Greenwood developed its own vibrant church community with Vernon African American Episcopal Church and Mt. Zion Baptist Church establishing large congregations and beautiful buildings that would showcase their prosperity and religious culture.

Early Pentecostal Revivals

The earliest known Pentecostal meeting in Tulsa took place in 1906, when the city was just beginning to develop. Revivals were not uncommon in those days, as Presbyterian and Methodist ministers established missions in the young city. However, a story in the June 1906 *Tulsa Daily World* noted that a minister named Reverend Lewis had set up a tent on 2nd and Main, the site of the historic Hotel Tulsa. Lewis' preaching was "accompanied by great power" and over a dozen people received salvations or sanctification. [6] While it remains unclear whether Lewis was Pentecostal, the paper advertised that Charles F. Parham,

---

[3] Hirsch, *Riot and Remembrance*, 34-35.

[4] Scott Ellsworth, *Death in a Promised Land: The Tulsa Race Riot of 1921* (Baton Rouge: University of Louisiana Press, 1982), 8-14.

[5] Hannibal B. Johnson, *Black Wallstreet: From Riot to Renaissance in Tulsa's Historic Greenwood District* (Austin, TX: Eakin Press, 1998).

[6] "The Big Tent Meeting," *The Morning Tulsa Daily World*, June 8, 1906, 1.

from Baxter Springs, would join Lewis later that month and was certain to bring "old fashioned revival" to town. By that time, Parham received regular press for his followers, who were known as "Holy Rollers" for emphasizing speaking in tongues. Most accounts, including his wife's biographical account, put Parham in Tulsa in 1908, not 1906.[7] Assuming he arrived there as advertised, this visit would have been on Parham's way back from preaching at the Houston Bible School, where William Seymour heard of the Pentecostal message. No doubt the success of the Houston ministry would have been shared in Tulsa, stirring up interest in the new doctrine of the baptism in the Holy Spirit.

We do know that in 1908, Parham was invited to come to Tulsa by Vandella (or Vandalia) Frye, wife of prominent Tulsa businessman, C. O. Frye.[8] Frye heard Parham speak about Pentecost in her hometown of Joplin, Missouri in 1901 and where she received the baptism in the Holy Spirit. When she and her husband moved to Tulsa in 1905, she found that she was the only person to have received the Pentecostal experience.[9] Frye held cottage prayer meetings in her home for those interested in the Apostolic Faith message. In the first few months, only three people received Pentecost in her home and Frye knew she needed to send for Parham to come to Tulsa to preach the Apostolic Faith message.

Sister Frye was extremely important to the early Pentecostal revival in Tulsa. In August 1908, she sold her diamond ring for $1,500 to secure Parham's band and invest in a tent for the revival.[10] In a tent set up at 3rd and Cincinnati, over a hundred people came to Christ and twelve received the baptism in the Holy Spirit

---

[7] Sarah Parham, *The Life of Charles F. Parham: Founder of the Apostolic Faith Movement* (Joplin, MO: The Tri-State Printing, 1930), 206. However, the date August 1908 is quoted from Mrs. C. O. Frye, rather than Sarah Parham. So it is possible that the 1908 date was wrong all along.

[8] It is interesting that most of the later accounts for Tulsa's Central Assembly (5th and Peoria) have the name "Vandalia Fry." However, her own testimonies sent to Pentecostal papers has her last name as "Mrs. C. O. Frye" and Ancestry.com records have her name as "Vandella M. A. Burke," married to "Charles O. Frye."

[9] "Tulsa, Oklahoma," *The Latter Rain*, 1908, Pauline Parham Collection, Oral Roberts University.

[10] "Journey Through Time," Central Assembly of God, Tulsa Oklahoma, 1997; Clarence B. Douglas, *The History of Tulsa, Oklahoma: A City with Personality* (Chicago: J. Clarke Publishing, 1921), 293, notes that it was 1908 that Parham came to Tulsa. This is disputed by the June 1906 *Tulsa World* report and the *60th Anniversary Celebration, Central Assembly of God Church*, 1968, Flower Pentecostal Heritage Center. It is also possible that Parham could have returned in 1908. This is doubtful, however, because Parham had fallen out of favor in many Pentecostal circles by 1908.

at the altar services. Some of the converts became the core group for what would eventually become 5th and Peoria Church. These included: Fannie Hughes, Mabel Hughes, Willa Lowther, Mr. and Mrs. A. J. Welker, Martha Baxter, E. K. Gray, Oscar Wolfe, Frank Carter, Mr. and Mrs. John Reddout, and Mrs. Sam Dague. A year later, Parham's sister-in-law, Lillian Thistlewaite, ministered in the city. One of her notable converts was Willard Pope, founder of the first Pentecostal church in Broken Arrow.

Not long after Parham's campaign, Frye leased a small former Methodist Church building at 2nd and Cincinnati to hold meetings three times a week. But she did not assume the preaching duties.[11] Instead, Frye reports, "[p]eople wonder how we have such meetings without a preacher, but when they come out, they see that we have many preacher[s], and the best of all we have the power of the Holy Spirit in all our meetings."[12] In September of 1908, Mrs. J. C. Ament attended one of the meetings where she was healed of blindness, spinal trouble, and gastritis. She proclaimed, "I have been perfectly well ever since."[13] She not only was healed, but she also received sanctification and was filled with the Holy Spirit. As she recalls:

> Oh such rest and peace! Such joy! Such heavenly divine sweetness filled my soul. Rivers of living water flowed through me. Volume after volume of love and power seemed to take full possession of body soul and spirit. ... I am praising Him continually for the real evidence of this Pentecostal baptism, not only speaking and singing in tongues, but for enduement of power to glorify Jesus and witness for Him.[14]

As attendance grew, the church looked for a permanent home. For a short time in 1909, they rented the old Indian Territory Courthouse next door on 2nd Street between Cincinnati and Detroit.[15] Finally, the Apostolic Faith Mission (taking on

---

[11] Frye's husband, C. O. Frye, owned a concrete business, the Tulsa Cement Stone Co., and was instrumental in building some of Tulsa's most famous buildings. Some accounts say she sold the ring to secure a tent for Parham to come. However, it is more likely that the money would have been needed to secure the building, rather than a tent.

[12] "Tulsa, Oklahoma," *The Latter Rain*, 1908, Pauline Parham Collection, Holy Spirit Research Center, Oral Roberts University, Tulsa, Oklahoma.

[13] Mrs. J. C. Ament, "Atrophied Optic Nerve, Spinal Trouble, and Gastritis Healed," *Latter Rain Evangel*, February 1909, 19-20.

[14] ibid., 20.

[15] *The Pentecost*, November 1, 1909, 4; *History of Tulsa*, 293.

the name of Parham's group) leased a lot on the corner of Brady and Cincinnati, at 115 E. 2nd Street/Brady, the current site of the Guthrie Green.

3.1 Indian Territory Courthouse, Tulsa

Over the next few years, Frye invited Pentecostal preachers to hold meetings to further the Apostolic Faith message. In 1909, A. S. Copley, editor of *The Pentecost*, had glowing reports of his ministry in the city and described the saints there as "happy, earnest and aggressive, yet so free from fleshly noise and energy." His ministry, he reported, was one of the most profitable of his life. He commented, "Sinners were saved, believers were sanctified, healed and baptized in the Holy Spirit. There were more cases of healing than I have witnessed in one meeting for several years."[16]

In the spring of 1911, L. P. Adams, a white minister who pastored a church in Memphis within Mason's Church of God in Christ, held revival services in Tulsa.[17] Another white COGIC minister, Charles Squire and his wife, Sarah, of Danville, Illinois, came to the city in October of that same year. The Squires were evangelists and songwriters who put out an early Pentecostal songbook called *Psalms, Hymns, and Spiritual Songs* with Shelley E. Kinnee.[18] They teamed with the Apostolic Mission to hold a tent meeting on 4th Street and Elgin, and reported, "God is wonderfully blessing. Precious souls are being saved and baptized in the Holy

---

[16] A. S. Copley, "Victory in Tulsa," *The Pentecost*, April 1909, 5.
[17] "Revivalist Returns Home," *The Morning Tulsa Daily World*, May 2, 1911, 8.
[18] "Pentecostal Song Book," *Bridegroom's Messenger*, November 15, 1910, 2.

Ghost and fire and speaking in tongues as they did on the day of Pentecost. Many are receiving healing from sickness."[19]

The early Pentecostal saints didn't just preach; they were active in the community. Several members of the Apostolic Faith Mission teamed with the Salvation Army to preach and distribute food at the county prison. Tulsa's famed Sherriff Newblock welcomed the Apostolic believers to visit on holidays and anytime they wished to preach.[20] In 1912, Frye's husband, Charles, a successful business leader in the community, ran for Mayor as a Republican.[21] In the early twentieth century, Republicans were the party of the lower class and had unsuccessfully resisted the Jim Crow takeover at statehood by Democrats four years earlier. Frye ran on the platform of lower taxes and better government but held progressive positions on wage reform and felt "every effort should be made to look after

3.2 Charles O. Frye

the welfare of our own laboring people." He employed low skill and low wage workers in the concrete business, and he recognized that reform was needed, writing,

> The present scale of wages at twenty-five cents per hour is too low and does not and will not buy for the laborer and his family the necessities of life. ... In the prosperity of our working people, in its fullness, is the measure of our commercial, industrial and moral progress.[22]

Although she resisted being called the pastor, Vandella Frye should be rightfully recognized as the founder of Pentecostalism in Tulsa. She not only brought Pentecost to Tulsa, but she shepherded the Pentecostal believers in the early years.

---

[19] "Tulsa, Oklahoma," *The Bridegroom's Messenger*, November 15, 1911, 2. See *Word and Witness*, December 20, 1913, 6. Squire died of leukemia on January 14, 1916, but Sarah Squire continued to minister and became an instructor at T. K. Leonard's Gospel School in Findlay, Ohio. See, "Elder Chas A. Squire Called Home," *Bridegroom's Messenger*, March 1, 1916, 2.

[20] "Have Good Dinner: County Prisoners Eat Well and Hear the Word Preached," *The Morning Tulsa Daily World*, December 28, 1910, 1.

[21] "Political Announcements," *The Morning Tulsa Daily World*, January 23, 1912, 4. This is not to be confused with the C. O. Frye from Chickasha, Oklahoma who was a noted lawyer during the same era.

[22] "C. O. Frye and What He Stands For," *The Morning Tulsa Daily World*, March 19, 1912, 3.

Through her faithful witness and sacrifice in pioneering this original mission, several other Pentecostal works were established.

Pentecost in Greenwood

It is unknown exactly when the first Black Pentecostal church began in Tulsa. Since we know that Oklahoma had at least two COGIC churches in 1910, one could have been in Tulsa. A 1921 *Polk Tulsa City Directory* indicates that a Church of God in Christ was founded in 1910 at 211 E. Independence, (near Cincinnati, known today as MLK Boulevard), just two blocks north and west of deep Greenwood.[23] The claim seems credible for a couple of reasons. First, it is reasonable to believe that Pentecostals were among the African Americans drawn to Greenwood's promising community. Second, the details about the other churches in the *Polk Directory* are accurate. The address and pastor's name as Allen Burgess, noted in the directory is different than the North Greenwood Church of God in Christ. Despite this convincing evidence, no COGIC materials corroborate this claim.

As was noted earlier, white COGIC ministers L. P. Adams and Charles Squire both came to Tulsa in 1911,[24] so the congregation might have been interracial or white. But the best evidence is its location. The white neighborhood, two blocks west of Greenwood, is not likely to have hosted a black church and the lack of additional information makes the 1910 date only speculation.

North Greenwood Church of God in Christ

According to several sources, the first black Pentecostal church in Tulsa was North Greenwood or First Church of God in Christ formally organized in 1917. However, its story begins in 1914 when Mother Lizzie Robinson, President of the National Women's Department, sent four women, Sister Fugett,

---

[23] *Polk-Hoffhine Directory Co.'s Tulsa City Directory* (1921), 15-16. The directory gives the date of its establishment as 1910, but no other details have been found in COGIC directories. It also names a pastor as Allen Burgess.

[24] "Revivalist Returns Home," *The Morning Tulsa Daily World*, May 2, 1911, 8.

Sister M. J. Elija, Sister Prescott, and Sister Warren to Tulsa to raise up a new work. As Anthea Butler, notes, COGIC Church Mothers pioneered churches and then recruited a man to fill the pastorate. Butler points out that some Tulsa ministers (presumably from other black denominations such as the AME) resisted the work.[25] However, these women preached the Pentecostal message and prepared the land for the North Greenwood church.

That year, Bishop C. H. Mason commissioned Bishop Page to visit the COGIC in Tulsa.[26] Seeing that the work was in need of encouragement and a permanent pastor, in 1917, Page asked a young pastor from Arkansas, Travis B. Sipuel, to serve as pastor. Sipuel was a brilliant man who excelled in organization and was particularly good at managing church finances. He leased a building at 700 N. Greenwood Avenue, nestled in the hill below the Brick Plant.[27] Today, this location is a parking lot north of Oklahoma State University-Tulsa. He called the church the North Greenwood Church of God in Christ, or Tulsa Mission #1. It later became known as First Church of God in Christ. Sipuel also rented a home on Greenwood Avenue for his wife and himself. They were excited about the potential of the city for a successful life and ministry, and Sipuel, a gifted leader, regularly canvased the neighborhood with flyers. The church quickly grew to forty people and 1921 had 250 members.[28] The church and Sipuel's family, however, would endure a huge trial, as we will cover later in this book.

5th and Peoria Mission

From 1908–1911, Sister Frye's Apostolic Faith Mission met in a storefront building at Brady and Cincinnati. As their lease was expiring in 1911, the congregation secured a lot at 115 E. North 2nd Street at the corner of Cincinnati and Brady

---

[25] Butler, *Women in the Church of God in Christ*, 51-52. The 1926 COGIC Yearbook indicates that M. J. Elija remained in Tulsa, serving as an evangelist.

[26] *Yearbook of the Church of God in Christ (1926)*, 67. Page comments he came to Tulsa and the church was "revived," indicating that the church already existed.

[27] Ada Lois Sipuel Fisher, *Matter of Black and White* (University of Oklahoma Press, 2006), 10.

[28] The *Polk-Hoffhine Directory Co.'s Tulsa City Directory* (1922) notes this as the second COGIC church in Tulsa, although it is hard to know if the two churches were related.

Street/Reconciliation Way.[29] In 1912, a 20' x 40' wood frame church was built. The city officials had adopted the name "Church of the Holy Rollers," a take-off of the title that had given to the followers of Parham in various newspapers.[30]

The next task was to seek out a permanent pastor for the congregation. The first pastor, David Hockersmith, served only for a short time[31] while Willard Pope, a young leader, helped out and preached from time to time. The first full-time pastor was W. T. Gaston (1886–1956), who had the biggest impact on the stability of the church when he arrived in Tulsa in 1912. In 1909, at age twenty-three, Gaston became an evangelist in Arkansas and gained the reputation as "the walking evangelist" because he literally walked all over state preaching the Pentecostal message. In 1910, Gaston came to Tahlequah to hold a revival, and stayed for two years as the pastor.

In 1912, Pope attended the Interstate campmeeting in Eureka Springs, Arkansas seeking a permanent pastor for the Tulsa work. Once there, he persuaded Gaston to pastor the Tulsa Mission.[32] Gaston was known for his anointed preaching and the miracles that were associated with his ministry. During the 1913 summer campmeeting, he reported, "Souls are weeping their way to the cross nearly every night Already some remarkable cases of healing. The other night God touched a poor old man who had been on a crutch for 4 years."[33]

Under Gaston's leadership, the church grew, but he began looking for a better site away from the downtown location. He and a deacon named "Daddy Reeder" chose a plot in a neighborhood on Peoria, south and east of downtown. Having just built the church on Brady and with little money to rebuild at the new location, they took the building with them. On a cold winter day in 1915, two mules dragged the 20' x 40' structure nearly a mile through mud and snow to 5th and Peoria. And, settled in their new location, the church thrived.

What was the motivation of this move? It may have been the beginning of "whiteflight" for Tulsa's white Pentecostals. Leroy Hawkins states that Frye's Brady

---

[29] Hawkins, "A History of the Assemblies of God in Oklahoma," 59

[30] This is the title on the 1915 Sanborn Fire Maps, local city maps that detail the buildings in Tulsa.

[31] Ibid., 61.

[32] Ibid., 49.

[33] W. T. Gaston, "Tulsa, Okla.," *Pentecostal Evangel*, August 20, 1913, 3.

and Cincinnati property was in a "poor location, near the railroad tracks," an insight that came from an interview with one of the members.[34] The railroad tracks were a dividing line between the black and white neighborhoods. Since the church was three blocks west of Greenwood, and Gaston's home address was 402 N. Elgin, next door to Mt. Zion Baptist Church, the white church members may have been growing uncomfortable in the growing Greenwood area. This is pattern has been repeated by white Pentecostal churches throughout Tulsa's history.

Nevertheless, the move was good for the church. Gaston's leadership of the congregation perfectly situated him to be elected the first District Superintendent of Oklahoma for the Assemblies of God in 1914. In this position, he made regular tours of the churches around the state encouraging revival. In 1916, he left Tulsa to pastor in the Southern Missouri District of the Assemblies of God. He went on to serve as the Assemblies of God General Superintendent from 1925–1929 and later, as Superintendent of the Northern California and Nevada Districts.[35]

The next pastor to come to Tulsa was Samuel A. Jamieson, perhaps equally important to the early Assemblies of God as Gaston. Jamieson, a well-educated Presbyterian pastor and a denominational leader before becoming a Pentecostal,[36] received the baptism in the Spirit under the ministry of Maria Woodworth-Etter in Texas in 1908.[37] His prior leadership, theological training, and passion for Pentecostal truths made him a logical choice as an AG Executive Presbyter. In 1917, the year after Jamieson became the pastor, he became the Oklahoma District Superintendent (1917–1920).[38] He was a member of the committee that crafted the Statement of Fundamental Truths in 1916 and its revision in 1927. He also published the first AG doctrinal book, *Pillars of Truth*, in 1926. AG historian, Carl Brumback, credits him with significantly "molding the conservative nature of the

---

[34] Hawkins, "A History of the Assemblies of God in Oklahoma," 58.

[35] "Another Pioneer Called Home," *Pentecostal Evangel*, September 30, 1956, 5.

[36] S. A. Jamieson, "How a Presbyterian Received the Baptism," January 31, 1931, 2. Jamieson graduated from Wabash College and Lane Theological Seminary.

[37] Glenn Gohr notes that Jamieson received the baptism in the Spirit in 1912; however, this contradicts Jamieson's own testimony, which cites 1908. Glenn Gohr, "An Early A/G Leader: Samuel A. Jamieson," *Assemblies of God Heritage* (February 1991): 9-10; Jamieson, "How a Presbyterian Received the Baptism," *Pentecostal Evangel*, January 31, 1931, 2.

[38] Gohr, "An Early A/G Leader," 9-10. In 1920, Jamieson was given the responsibility of starting the first General Council Bible School in Auburn, Nebraska. After it failed, he took up a pastorate in Chicago and became the Illinois District Superintendent.

Assemblies of God." [39] Jamieson was followed in the pastorate by E. G. Cunningham (1919–1920).[40]

Apostolic Faith State Encampment

Beginning around 1910, a debate over sanctification as a "second work of grace" divided the Pentecostal Movement into two camps. The Holiness-Pentecostal stream emphasized the Wesleyan-Holiness view of sanctification as a definite work of grace prior to Spirit baptism. This position was held by most early Pentecostals including Charles Parham, William Seymour, C. H. Mason, G. B. Cashwell, and J. H. King. This three-fold view of grace was essential to the earliest Holiness-Pentecostal groups, including the COGIC, Pentecostal Holiness, and Church of God (Cleveland, TN). Another stream, emerging in Parham's circles in the Midwest, saw sanctification as a "finished work" that occurred at salvation, rather than a second work. These more Baptist or Reformed believers were influenced by the Keswick stream of the Holiness movement. They emphasized only two works of grace: salvation and baptism in the Holy Spirit with the evidence of speaking in tongues.

While many Pentecostals operated in both circles, the differences in theology caused issues between the two camps. This was first seen when Glen A. Cook came into conflict with King in Lamont in 1907 over sanctification. But William Durham caused a schism in the Pentecostal Movement when he openly challenged Seymour's view of sanctification in 1912. [41] Durham and his Finished Work message became the dominant position of Pentecostals in Oklahoma, Texas, and Arkansas, championed by noted Pentecostal leaders Howard Goss, E. N. Bell, M. M. Pinson, A. P. Collins, and F. F. Bosworth.

That year, when Durham died unexpectedly, Bell and Goss, with their previous leadership of Parham's networks, were perfectly positioned to step in and hold

---

[39] S. A. Jamieson, *Pillars of Truth* (Springfield, MO: Gospel Publishing House, 1926). Carl Brumback, *Like a River* (Springfield, MO: Gospel Publishing House, 1977), 134.

[40] The Central Assembly History, "Journey Through Time," includes a full list of pastors.

[41] Edith L. Blumhofer, "William H. Durham: Years of Creativity, Years of Dissent," in *Portraits of a Generation*, ed. James R. Goff Jr. and Grant Wacker (Fayetteville, AR: University of Arkansas Press, 2002), 123-42.

together this Finished Work camp. However, they wanted to abandon the Apostolic Faith label after Parham was embroiled in scandal and did not want to be associated with the divisiveness of Durham's Finished Work label.[42] So in 1912, Goss was commissioned to seek Mason's permission to issue credentials under the Churches of God in Christ.[43] During 1912–1914, 300 white ministers were ordained in COGIC and held annual state camp meetings in Texas, Arkansas, and Oklahoma. One popular destination for these meetings was Tulsa.

When Gaston came to Frye's Apostolic Faith Mission, Tulsa became the logical center for gathering the saints in Eastern Oklahoma. In 1912, he invited Goss and Bell to have the Oklahoma State Encampment in Tulsa. In attendance were Goss, Pope, Gaston, L. C. Hall, and M. M. Pinson. The next year, the State Encampment was held at Orcutt Lake Park, in a wealthy area south of downtown now called Swan Lake (21st and Utica).[44] As a city social hub on the southernmost stop of the cable car line, the park hosted a lake for swimming and fishing, a beautiful picnic area, and an amusement park with a roller coaster.[45] During the three-week long tent campmeeting, Gaston recalls:

> The power of God increased from day to day until the ninth day when the glory of the Lord over-shadowed the camp, and wave after wave of power and glory swept over the vast audience. Some cried and shouted, while others, like David of old, danced before the Lord.[46]

---

[42] E. N. Bell, "Notice About Parham," *Word and Witness*, October 1910, 3. See also Goss, *Winds of God*, 168.

[43] Since Parham's group did not issues credentials, Goss approached Charles Mason about issuing credentials under the "Churches of God in Christ." For a list of all the ministers ordained under the Churches of God in Christ prior to the first General Council. See *Word and Witness*, December 20, 1913, 4.

[44] "'Holy Rollers' Camp Meeting on Today," *Tulsa Daily World*, July 22, 1914, 5, mentions the previous years the meeting was held at Orcutt Lake Park.

[45] Colonel Samuel Orcutt was one of the first white settlers to the Tulsa area and was instrumental in its establishment as a town. Nancy [No last name given on blog], "The Orcutt Family," Tulsa Gal Blog, July 1, 2009, accessed December 15, 2020, http://www.tulsagal.net/2009/07/orcutt-family.html.

[46] W. T. Gaston, "Refreshing Times at Oklahoma Camp," *Word and Witness*, September 20, 1913, 1.

The meetings celebrated thirty-six water baptisms and over forty Spirit-baptisms and Gaston reports: "The other night, God touched the body of a poor old man who had been on a crutch four years. He threw away his crutch."[47]

The success of the Encampment led to an important move by Bell and Goss, who along with Daniel Opperman, published an announcement of a General Council to take place in Hot Springs Arkansas the next April to officially form the General Council of the Assemblies of God. The notice read, "To all the churches of God in Christ, to all Pentecostal or Apostolic Faith Assemblies who desire to with united propose to cooperate in love …"[48]

Three months later, in July 2014, Tulsa hosted the Oklahoma State Encampment. This time they set up camp on the banks of the Arkansas River at Midway/Assembly Park near "Joe Station" stop on the Sand Springs Line. Although the exact location is unclear, it was likely on the banks of the Arkansas River along Charles Page Boulevard between New Block Park and the old Tulsa Waterworks building.[49] The wealthy founder of Sand Springs, Charles Page, built a large 80' x 100' tabernacle costing $3,000 for the Pentecostal community and renamed the park "Assembly Park."[50] Though not a Pentecostal, Page was often involved in various philanthropy projects including building several churches.[51]

During the meeting, the saints organized the Oklahoma District of the Assemblies of God, as the first statewide AG district. Gaston was elected State Chairman, making Tulsa the headquarters for Oklahoma AG. The ten-day meeting

---

[47] Gaston, "Tulsa, Okla.," *Word and Witness*, August 20, 1913, 3.

[48] "General Convention of Pentecostal Saints and Churches of God in Christ," *Word and Witness*, December 1912, 1.

[49] The Sand Springs Car Line was established by Charles Page in 1911 encouraged travelers to come to Page's newly established park. Joe Station was located on the line on 25th West Avenue. The previous stop was Newblock Station, likely the site of the present Newblock Park. See Tulsa County Board of Commissioners, "Charles Page Boulevard Area Neighborhood Revitalization Plan," November 4, 1996, Appendix A, Tulsa Planning Office, accessed August 27, 2020, http://tulsaplanning.org/wp-content/uploads/2019/06/charles-page-plan.pdf.

[50] "'Holy Rollers' Camp Meeting on Today," *Tulsa Daily World*, July 22, 1914, 5; "Annual Encampment of Pentecostal Saints for the State of Oklahoma," *Christian Evangel*, July 25, 1914, 2; T. K. Leonard, "My Summer Camp Meeting Tour," *Christian Evangel*, September 19, 1914, 1. It is unclear if it was named "assembly" because of the Assembly of God or just the general term "assembly."

[51] See Opal B. Clark, *A Fool's Enterprise: The Life of Charles Page* (Sand Springs, OK: Dexter Publishing, 2001).

was attended by hundreds including future AG leaders A. P. Collins, T. K. Leonard, Howard Goss, J. W. Welch, and J. H. James. The report was that:

> During those meetings the altar was crowded about every meeting, with twenty to forty earnest seekers [of the baptism in the Holy Spirit]. Many were saved and baptized in the Holy Ghost. Many professed healing, and a blessed unity of the saints was manifested. Especially we commend the saints for the blessed unity.[52]

3.4 1914 Oklahoma State Encampment (IFPHC)

The saints were pleased that the Oklahoma camp was marked by such unity in the Spirit after the division of the finished work controversy in the years before. Yet, conspicuously absent were black Pentecostals from Greenwood.

Mission of Redeeming Love

Fueled with a burden for the hurting in the streets of Tulsa, sometime around 1910, M. Simpson Allen recruited several of the city's businessmen to help establish a mission where people could find "refuge from the storms of life." He called it, The Mission of Redeeming Love, which was located at 109 E. 2nd Street. Joining him was Mrs. L. A. Newberry, who had experience in opening rescue homes for wayward street girls.[53] Together they served Tulsa's poor, needy and down and out.

---

[52] T. K. Leonard, "My Summer Camp Meeting Tour," *Christian Evangel*, September 19, 1914, 1.
[53] Douglas, *History of Tulsa*, 297.

Whether the mission was Pentecostal in the early days is unclear. In June of 1913, however, when Allen and Newberry moved to St. Louis to start new homes. Minnie B. Hiland, a Pentecostal, came from Pittsburgh take the leadership of the home. Under her leadership, the Mission held Pentecostal revivals in addition to their humanitarian work.[54] In 1917, a group of businessmen funded a new four-story mission at 107 S. Boston. One Jewish convert, Morris Kullman, joined the Assemblies of God and opened the Messianic Jewish Mission in St. Louis in 1921.[55] The congregation continued on as a Pentecostal mission until the 1950s.

The Apostolic (Oneness) Church

In 1915, the Pentecostal community faced the challenge of the "New Issue."—the Trinitarian-Oneness schism. The controversy centered on whether the Apostolic pattern for baptism in water was to be in "Jesus' name" or according to the Trinitarian formula. Glenn Cook, who was first to endorse the Finished Work theology, now endorsed baptism in Jesus' name. In 1915, Cook re-baptized Garfield T. Haywood and the Pentecostal Assemblies of the World embraced the new Oneness identity. Several prominent Assemblies of God minsters, including Bell, Goss, Opperman, Frank Ewart, and William Booth-Clibborn moved into the Oneness camp. In 1916 as tensions surrounding the Oneness doctrine rose, the AG made a definitive stand for Trinitarian theology by establishing the Statement of Fundamental Truths. These statements forced many Oneness ministers out the denomination. Some formed a new General Assembly of Apostolic Assemblies that merged with the Pentecostal Assemblies of the World a year later. While the camps share a common heritage back to Parham's visit in 1908, the controversy hindered Apostolic congregations in Tulsa. The first congregation was not established until 1922 by Arthur Duck. That story will be told in a later chapter.

---

[54] For example, the *Tulsa Weekly Democrat*, July 31, 1913, 3, reports that Evangelist B. W. Huckabee of Texas came to the Mission and preached "the genuine old time power and fire."

[55] Morris Kullman, *Matthew 12:40* (Tulsa, OK: Morris Kullman, 1924); Digital Showcase (Oral Roberts University), accessed December 15, 2020, https://digitalshowcase.oru.edu/hsbooks/7/. "Opening of a Jewish Mission in St. Louis," *Pentecostal Evangel*, June 25, 1921, 16.

In 1916, William Moore pastored the Apostolic Church in Broken Arrow, the only Oneness congregation in the town. Though the congregation was often the target of criticism and was severely persecuted, Moore was a regular speaker in Tulsa and in Jenks. His example, though severe, illustrates the hostility some Pentecostals faced during this period. In May 1916, he and several members of his church received death threats. A few weeks later, their building was burned to the ground. Witnessing the church in flames, Moore tried to save it, but was confronted by the perpetrators, who shot and wounded him slightly on his scalp and shoulder. After Moore lay bleeding on the nearby railroad track until someone found him, he recovered and resumed preaching, traveling to Tulsa on June 9. This was the last time anyone heard from Moore. Several weeks later, the police discovered his body in the Arkansas River.[56]

---

[56] "Identify Drowned Man as Preacher," *Morning Tulsa World*, June 25, 1916, 3. The history of Broken Arrow Assembly notes that their first church also burned in 1916. Likely, this was a separate Oneness Pentecostal church This makes it likely that both churches were persecuted by citizens of Broken Arrow that year.

4

PENTECOST IN GREEN COUNTRY

The City of Tulsa holds together a larger community of suburbs and small towns in the greater Green Country area that have always been interconnected with the Tulsa community. Today, some of these communities, such as Broken Arrow, Bixby, and Jenks, are hardly discernable from where the city ends, and they begin. In the 1910s and 1920s, these were separate communities. Many of them have their own significant histories, and a brief look at the Pentecostal works in these areas is beneficial.

Bartlesville

Situated in Osage County north of Tulsa, Bartlesville is the home of famed oil man, Frank Phillips. It was also an important location for Pentecostals in Green Country. In the spring of 1921, when Mrs. Adeline Godwin of Bartlesville went to Colorado to visit her brother, she received the baptism in the Holy Ghost at an Assemblies of God church. Returning home, Godwin started holding prayer meetings in her home for her friends and relatives. In 1922, A. B. Harmon and J. L. Nevills came to Bartlesville to hold revival meetings at 2nd Street and Osage, with good results. But it was the 1923 revivals at the Old Candy Kitchen on Park Street that really had an impact, as over 1,100 people received Christ. The evangelists also reportedly prayed for 1,700 sick people. Nevills writes, "The saints are needing an assembly for the full gospel, but there is much opposition. Pray that the work shall be organized here and a real man of God [be] sent as pastor."[1] In December, Nevills helped organize a Sunday school with 108 people in attendance, but as opposition continued to grow, he wrote, "This is a new field, and the prospects are good for a church; but the battle is hot, but we are crying, 'Lord, send rain.'"[2]

The prayer for a permanent Pentecostal church in Bartlesville was answered when J. M. Kerr established an Assemblies of God church on May 1, 1924 and built a building on 1025 W. 3rd Street. Pastor H. E. Bowley of the 5th and Peoria congregation helped open the church and notes: "At the very first service, the house was filled with hungry people, many of whom were seeking the baptism in the Holy Spirit, and we bespeak a wonderful future under the blessing of God for Bartlesville."[3] The church continued to have great success with many people saved, healed and baptized in the Holy Spirit.

4.1 Bartlesville Assembly of God 1920s

Bartlesville was a favorite destination for itinerate Pentecostal Holiness Church evangelists. Between 1923–1924, G. B. Tims pastored Bartlesville Pentecostal Holiness Church. Evangelist E. G. Murr said of Tims, "He sure is a fine pastor

---

[1] "Bartlesville, Okla.," *Pentecostal Evangel*, November 10, 1923, 11.

[2] "Bartlesville, Okla.," *Pentecostal Evangel*, January 12, 1924, 8.

[3] "Bartlesville, Okla.," *Pentecostal Evangel*, April 26, 1924, 12.

and knows how to keep things together."[4] Noted Oklahoma PH preachers such as O. C. Wilkins, M. L. Dryden, and Dan Evans loved to visit Bartlesville. E. M. Orffutt commented, "There is some true gold there. ... It always does my soul good to see the saints working like they are at Bartlesville." [5] Dan Muse also observed, "This church certainly has some live wires in it that are filled with the 'go tell it' message of salvation... They are determined that everybody within their reach is going to hear or read about this Gospel." [6] The church was known for its commitment to holiness teachings. As O. C. Wilkins comments, though, the Bartlesville believers were not just poor and ignorant. He boasted,

> Some of them are bookkeepers, some cashiers, some musicians and some are stenographers and I don't know one of them that is grown that has her hair bobbed, or that wears jewelry or that come to the church with their arms naked, and I don't know of a more intelligent congregation anywhere than this one.[7]

After several years of leadership by Tims, B. R. Dean became the pastor in 1925.

Bixby

Bixby was a government township established in 1902. It was named after Tams Bixby, a member of the 1893 Dawes Commission. Bixby was a stop on the route between Tulsa and Muskogee along the Arkansas River. Originally, there were several ferries to cross the river, but in 1911, a bridge was built on what is today Riverside Street (between Memorial and Mingo). The Bixby bridge helped establish the town and unified the various surrounding area communities of Frye, Willow Creek, and Shellenbarger.

The first church in Bixby was a Missionary Baptist Church built in 1903 at the corner of Main and Breckenridge. But by 1915, the town had its first known Pentecostal community. The *Bixby Bulletin* reports that "the ministerial force of the

---

[4] "The Meeting at Bartlesville," *The Pentecostal Holiness Faith*, January 15, 1923, 2.
[5] "Reports of Meetings," *The Pentecostal Holiness Faith*, November 15, 1922, 5.
[6] "Eastern Oklahoma Conference," *The Pentecostal Holiness Faith*, October 1, 1924, 5.
[7] O. C. Wilkins, "Reports from the Field," *The Pentecostal Holiness Faith*, July 15, 1925, 6.

'Holy Rollers'" were working on building a church building.[8] The Pentecostal believers (possibly Oneness) had a significant mission in Bixby. In April, they held a baptism service in the Arkansas River, and many were baptized.[9] During the summer, a prolonged campmeeting added many believers; fifteen of whom were baptized on the Arkansas River.[10]

4.2 Baptism in the Arkansas River (Bixby Historical Society)

By early 1916, the Pentecostal church was gaining popularity among the churches in the community.[11] A few months later, the Pentecostal Church began meeting in a storefront in the Bramble Building.[12] The new building saw many converts added to the church. By the end of the month, the congregation baptized fifty new believers in the Arkansas River.[13]

---

[8] "Local Items," *Bixby Bulletin,* January 8, 1915, 6. This mentions that they left a building half built, but apparently that was only temporary.

[9] "Jenks Items," *Bixby Bulletin,* April 9, 1915, 3.

[10] "Local Items," *Bixby Bulletin,* June 25, 1915, 6.

[11] "The Community," *Bixby Bulletin,* March 31, 1916, 5. The list of churches included: The Christian Church, General Baptist, Missionary Baptist, M. E. Church, M. E. Church South, and Pentecostal Church.

[12] *Bixby Bulletin,* April 14, 1916, 1.

[13] "Pentecostal Meeting," *Bixby Bulletin,* April 21, 1916, 3.

Beginning in 1920, the Assemblies of God was established in Bixby under the ministry of noted Oklahoma evangelist, Pearl Watts.[14] Assemblies of God Pastor, J. E. Chamless, led the church while teaming with Watts to also start a mission in Jenks.[15] Richard M. Phillips, co-editor of the *Bixby Bulletin* was important member of the church. He came to Bixby in 1908 to partner with W. W. Stuckey to publish the paper.[16] Phillips was a member of the church and was known for his sincere faith and Christian love. He often shared positive news about the Pentecostal group in the paper. Tragically, he died in a car accident in 1923.

Not everything related to the Bixby Pentecostal community was positive, particularly when related to the enthusiasm their worship services. F. E. Conrad opened a promising campmeeting in town on August 18, 1921, that quickly turned tragic. During a time of ecstatic praise, an attendee, Frank McCormick, fell on his one-year-old child. The church gathered to pray for the child, but the child died. The *Tulsa World* reported, news of the child's death was "[s]preading over the town with uncanny swiftness [and] wrought the citizens to a fever heat. When a mob formed and was going to teach the Holy Rollers a lesson,"[17] three citizens, including Mayor J. W. Stilts, protected the group. The Pentecostals fled the town until things calmed down. When they returned a year later, more trouble arose from the church when E. B. Baker was charged with an "alleged disturbance at the Holy Roller Church" in April 1922. Though the case went to trial, he was found not guilty.[18]

In May 1923, another Pentecostal mission was started in Bixby, and a revival was held on Breckenridge Avenue next to the telephone office.[19] The front page of the *Bixby Bulletin*, declared, "The sick are being prayed for and anointed with oil, and the Lord is healing."[20] The church was a member of the Oneness denomination, Pentecostal Assemblies of the World. It was pastored by W. L.

---

[14] "Revival," *Bixby Bulletin*, February 6, 1920, 3.

[15] "Bixby and Jenks," *Pentecostal Revival*, March 20, 1920, 14.

[16] "R. M. Phillips Killed in Auto Accident," *Bixby Bulletin*, December 14, 1923, 1.

[17] "Dismisses Riot Charge," *Bixby Bulletin*, September 23, 1921, 6; "Holy Rollers Cause Tragedy at Religious Meeting," *Tulsa Daily World*, September 4, 1921, 1.

[18] "Local Items," *Bixby Bulletin*, April 7, 1922, 5.

[19] "Pentecostal Mission," *Bixby Bulletin*, June 8, 1923, 1.

[20] "Pentecostal Revival," *Bixby Bulletin*, May 23, 1923, 1.

Schuessler, who held services every Saturday and Sunday night as well as a Thursday night prayer meeting.[21] Besides pastoring the congregation, he opened several businesses including a mattress company and the People's Market on Dawes near the post office.[22]

Broken Arrow

Today, Broken Arrow is one of Tulsa's largest suburbs. It began as a Creek Indian settlement following the removal of Native Americans from Alabama and Georgia on the Trail of Tears. The name comes from the tradition of breaking an arrow when a peace deal is made. By 1880, the town had become a white settlement, but continued to use the name the Creeks had given it. It was officially incorporated in 1902. Some of the earliest churches in the area were Indian missions established by the Presbyterians and Methodists, including the historic White Church on 129th and 121st Street.[23]

Pentecost first came to Broken Arrow in 1912 when Willard Pope held a revival there. Pope was saved in 1909 when Charles Parham's sister-in-law, Lillian Thistlewaite, held a revival in Tulsa. He quickly became a leader at the 5th and Peoria mission. One night as he was preaching in Tulsa, young Bill Williams was saved. Shortly after, Williams moved to Broken Arrow and invited Pope there to hold a tent meeting. [24] Though only nineteen, on arriving, Pope rented a tent in downtown that the Methodists had just finished using, so he could hold revival meetings. The local paper reported the great success of "The Pentecostal band [that] is holding forth at the tent near the Southern Methodist Church."[25] Further

---

[21] It is likely that his was a white P.A.W. church. By 1923, some of the white members of the P.A.W. were breaking off to start all-white Oneness groups. However, there certainly were blacks living in the Bixby area, especially in the Snake Creek community between Bixby and Leonard, which was an all-black community.

[22] "Local Items," *Bixby Bulletin,* July 18, 1924, 4. Schuessler moved in July 1924 to Albany, Texas.

[23] Donald E. Wise, "Broken Arrow," *Encyclopedia of Oklahoma History Online,* Oklahoma Historical Society, accessed November 8, 2020, https://www.okhistory.org/publications/enc/entry.php?entry=BR019.

[24] *Broken Arrow Assembly of God 75th Anniversary* (Broken Arrow, OK: 1992) Thanks to Stephanie Simon, Administrative Assistant at the Assembly at Broken Arrow for providing her research.

[25] Hawkins, "A History of the Assemblies of God in Oklahoma," 66.

they noted that the meeting had "quite a good many converts" and that "[s]ome of them make a good deal of noise and the meetings continue into the night."[26]

Pope established the church, but knowing he was in over his head as an inexperienced young minister, he invited several early leaders to preach to his fledgling congregation. One was M. M. Pinson, who in December of 1912 held a revival for Pope. Pinson lived in Malvern, Arkansas and helped lead the white COGIC churches with E. N. Bell. Pinson was an effective evangelist. Pope notes, "For the last three nights 16 have received the baptism. The town and county were stirred as never before."[27] Pinson returned in the summer of 1913 to once again hold revival for Pope.[28] In April, Pope traveled to Hot Springs to attend the first General Council of the Assemblies of God.

In 1914, Pope built a small church at 305 N. Main. While persecution was strong in the community, people came to hear the gospel. In 1916, Pope moved to Pawhuska, and M. M. Pinson returned to Broken Arrow to serve as pastor.[29] Later that year, the original building burned down and was rebuilt.[30] The church officially affiliated with the Assemblies of God in 1917. Other early pastors included Peter Davis, George Carriger, Joe Rosselli, Will Jones, and J. R. Evans.[31] In 1919, Pope returned to Broken Arrow from pastoring in Pawhuska and built a new building, which opened in April. At the dedication were J. W. Welch, the Superintendent of the Assemblies of God, and S. A. Jamieson, pastor of the 5th and Peoria Church. Pope held a two-month revival following the dedication, and many converts joined the young church. Pope declared, "God is blessing in the work and souls are being saved in almost every service."[32] In 1920, Paul C. Bucher became the pastor. He commented, "Although this is not a wealthy place, the saints, under the direction

---

[26] *Broken Arrow Assembly of God 75th Anniversary*, 13, Quoting *Broken Arrow Ledger*, August 22, 1912.

[27] "Broken Arrow, Okla.," *Word and Witness*, October 10, 1912, 2.

[28] "Broken Arrow, Okla.," *Word and Witness*, September 20, 1913, 3.

[29] "Oklahoma State Camp Meeting," *The Weekly Evangel*, June 17, 1916, 13.

[30] Lori Lewis, "Assembly Had Humble Beginnings," *Tulsa World*, May 26, 2016, accessed November 22, 2020, https://tulsaworld.com/the-assembly-had-humble-beginnings/article_c70298f6-bd79-57c7-807a-458d35538e40.html.

[31] Hawkins, "A History of the Assemblies of God in Oklahoma," 68.

[32] "Broken Arrow, Oklahoma," *Christian Evangel*, April 19, 1919, 13.

of Bro. W. H. Pope, have built a nice little chapel and parsonage, all furnished. The buildings are painted, and the saints are doing their part to advance the work of the Lord."[33]

4.3 Broken Arrow Assembly c. 1940 (The Assembly at Broken Arrow)

Bucher stayed only a year, leaving the church without a pastor until R. F. Smith arrived in early 1922. Smith reported having tremendous results in his revival writing, "There is victory in Broken Arrow. The Lord has saved 87 and baptized 46 with the Holy Spirit. Some wonderful healings."[34] The church grew with the community, becoming one of the most prominent AG churches in the area and a pillar of Broken Arrow. James C. Dodd came in 1946 and served for thirty-six years. He was responsible for building the new facility that was a staple on Main Street for many years.

---

[33] "Broken Arrow, Okla.," *The Pentecostal Evangel*, February 7, 1920, 10.
[34] "Broken Arrow, Okla.," *The Pentecostal Evangel*, March 4, 1922, 14.

Claremore

In 1915, Willard Pope came to Claremore hoping to establish a Pentecostal work. Pope began holding meetings and soon nearly forty people were added to the church.[35] A few months later, F. O. Burnett was chosen to shepherd the young flock.[36] For four years, the church struggled until C. M. Riggs held meetings in Claremore in 1919. Riggs' meetings strengthened the struggling church. He helped set the church in order with the Assemblies of God and appointed A. R. Donaldson as pastor.[37] In February, he went to nearby Catoosa and found hungry saints waiting for his message. He writes, "The altar was filled with hungry souls seeking for the old time Pentecostal baptism in the Spirit."[38] The meetings were so successful that Riggs invited District Chairman S. A. Jamieson to set the assembly in order.

In April, Donaldson hosted the annual Oklahoma District Council in Claremore. During the meeting, the Oklahoma churches planned the State campmeeting to feature Aimee Semple McPherson to be held at the Tulsa Convention Hall. This meeting was a boost for the fledgling Claremore Pentecostal community. G. G. Collins took over for Donaldson in the early 1920s, and later A. L. Steadman moved the church to a building downtown. In April 1926, Steadman held a revival led by Sister Eula Kellogg, reporting,

> Souls are being born into the kingdom and are being filled with the Holy Ghost. The town is stirred. We are worshipping in an old store building which will seat about 300 and the building is filled to its capacity and some have to stand in the aisle. We are planning on building in the near future.[39]

Revivals continued to be a catalyst for the growth of the church, and women had a lot to do with that growth—so much so that in 1928, Cora Crank served as Pastor and held revivals with evangelist Ruth Thompson.[40]

---

[35] "Nearly Forty Saved," *Weekly Evangel*, March 27, 1915, 2.
[36] "Claremore, Okla.," *Weekly Evangel*, June 26, 1915, 1.
[37] "Claremore, Okla.," *Christian Evangel*, March 8, 1919, 14.
[38] "Catoosa, Okla.," *Christian Evangel*, March 22, 1919, 14.
[39] "Claremore Stirred," *Pentecostal Evangel*, April 3, 1926, 12.
[40] "Claremore Revival," *Pentecostal Evangel*, January 28, 1928, 12.

Jenks

As early as 1915, Pentecostals from Bixby held meetings in nearby Jenks.[41] Several Pentecostal baptisms took place along the south side of the river, between the two communities and a few years later, the Pentecostal work in Jenks was founded by Pearl Watts. In February Watts reported about the Jenks work, "Have just started a meeting in the place, the house is filled every service."[42] J. E. Chamless pastored the new believers in Jenks.

In June 1922, a Pentecostal Holiness mission was started by Tulsa residents, T. E. and Lela Rhea, who had been working in Bristow with little success. T. E. testified, "When I first preached at Jenks, the little church was in bad shape."[43] After starting a Sunday school, they had five classes and the church was growing. They also started making repairs to the building and bought a piano. In 1923, a wild fire swept through the town, destroying the church, and many of the Pentecostal believers went elsewhere. But in 1926, Evangelist W. O. Singletary held a revival that "swept 26 souls into the kingdom and re-united the saints."[44] In June 1930, James Hutsell organized the remaining twenty believers into First Assembly of God in Jenks.[45]

Sand Springs

The community of Sand Springs lies along the Arkansas River, about five miles west of Tulsa. In 1912, philanthropist Charles Page established a children's home and created the town to support it. The extremely generous man helped fund many philanthropic projects in Tulsa and Sand Springs. He was not a church-going man, but he had a heart to help people, especially pastors.

The earliest Pentecostal church in Sand Springs, the Church of God in Christ was established in 1914, likely before Tulsa had a church. Most of the African

---

[41] "Jenks Items," *Bixby Bulletin*, April 9, 1915, 3.
[42] "Jenks, Okla.," The Pentecostal Evangel, February 7, 2020, 14.
[43] "New Sunday Schools," *The Pentecostal Holiness Faith*, July 1, 1922, 4.
[44] "Twenty-Six Converted," *Pentecostal Evangel*, April 24, 1926, 13.
[45] "Brief Mention," *Pentecostal Evangel*, June 14, 1930, 13.

Americans in Sand Springs lived in the segregated "colored town" where Page established the all-black Booker T. Washington High School. In 1921, Elder Malachi Green was listed in the *Polk City Directory* as the pastor of the "(Colored) Church of God" at 26 W. Pecan, on the major road between Sand Springs and West Tulsa along the Arkansas River. Though called "Church of God," COGIC sources identify Green as a notable ordained minister, so this was a COGIC congregation.

In August 1923, Green and several others from his church left Oklahoma to help pioneer the first church in Minnesota.[46] Green later became the first overseer for Minnesota COGIC churches and William G. Strassner, who also served in Tulsa, followed Green in leading the church in Sand Springs.

In 1913 and 1914, the summer campmeetings were held between Sand Springs and Tulsa, along the Arkansas River. People from Sand Springs attended the meetings and eventually started their own Pentecostal mission in the town. In June 1917, some Pentecostal believers invited Arkansas evangelists C. M. Riggs and Jenny Lind to hold a revival. Riggs reports: "God was with us in power, saving, healing and baptizing with the Holy Ghost. Fifty were saved and reclaimed. Twenty-three received the baptism of the Holy Ghost with evidence of speaking in tongues."[47] S. A. Jamieson, chairman of the Oklahoma AG, came to Sand Springs to organize the church. The revival continued through the fall. Charles Page was personally responsible for establishing the Sand Springs First Assembly of God in 1917.[48] He donated a piece of land that was being used as cattle pasture to build the first church, a building that was little more than a concrete slab and a roof for a tabernacle that held wooden benches for about fifty people. The members chose C. O. Higgins to be the first pastor.

Page was also involved with building a Pentecostal Holiness Bible school in Sand Springs. In 1927, King's College in Checotah was outgrowing its facility and Dan W. Evans began looking for a location to build a Bible school. Page gave them

---

[46] "Church of God in Christ, Minnesota (1923-2007)," *Church of God in Christ 100th International Holy Convocation* (Memphis, TN: COGIC, 2007), 870.

[47] "Sand Springs, Okla.," *Pentecostal Evangel,* June 30, 1917, 14.

[48] Josh Combs, "History of First Assembly of God," October 20, 1993, Church Vertical File, Sand Springs Museum, Sand Springs, Oklahoma.

land in Sand Springs but, within a few days of signing the deal, passed away. While college leaders feared that the school's future was in jeopardy, Page had already made arrangements to fund the project. Dan W. Evans rejoiced that God had already heard their prayers.[49] However, a few months later, the college elected a new president who chose to locate the institution in Kingfisher, Oklahoma.[50]

Sapulpa

Sapulpa, a community south and west of Tulsa in Creek County, was established by Creek tribal members who were re-settled from Alabama in the 1850s.[51] It was officially incorporated in 1898. The community began to grow after the discovery of oil in 1905 and the extension of the Tulsa rail line into Sapulpa. After statehood, Sapulpa became an important community, as the home of Creek County and later, as a stopping point along historic Route 66.

Sapulpa is thought to have one of the earliest COGIC churches in the area. In 1917, E. M. Page held a revival there and a COGIC church was established on 431 N. Leonard Street, where it stands today. While the early pastors are not known, Moses Griffin was the pastor in 1926, and later the church was pastored by notable Tulsa COGIC leader, J. L. (Jesse Lee) Alaman.

Another early Pentecostal work in Sapulpa was a Pentecostal Rescue Home in 1917 started by R. L. Cotham, the State Overseer for the Church of God in Oklahoma.[52] The ten-room Rescue Home at 15 N. Elm in downtown welcomed women and children who were in need.[53] It also held regular Pentecostal services and had a Bible school. One convert, Blanch Darner, testified in the *Church of God Evangel* that she was discipled under finished work Pentecostals, but discovered the truth of sanctification at the Mission. After her experience, she joined in rescuing

---

[49] King's College Location," *The Pentecostal Holiness Faith*, April 1, 1927, 7.
[50] "King's College to be Located in Kingfisher," *The Pentecostal Holiness Faith*, June 1, 1927, 1.
[51] James W. Hubbard, "Sapulpa," *The Encyclopedia of Oklahoma History and Culture*, accessed September 5, 2020, https://www.okhistory.org/publications/enc/entry.php?entry=SA021.
[52] "Pentecostal Rescue Home," *Weekly Evangel*, January 20, 1917, 15; *Church of God Evangel*, December 14, 1918, 2.
[53] "Pentecostal Rescue Home," *Pentecostal Evangel*, January 20, 1917, 15.

women and children from prostitution and human trafficking.[54] She writes, "The Lord has wonderfully put His approval upon the church here in the Rescue Home and unity prevails and souls are coming through to victory."[55] The church itself reported only fourteen members, but the work still had an impact on the community.[56]

Skiatook

In 1915, twelve-year-old, "Little Georgie Bynum" testified that his whole family had received the baptism in the Holy Spirit except his mama. He asked *Pentecostal Evangel* readers to pray that she would receive the baptism and that God would use him in the work.[57] Soon, Skiatook saw more people join the Pentecostals, but not everyone accepted the exuberant new Christian group. The Apostolic Faith Church in Skiatook made local news as locals were saying the nightly services were disturbing the peace. One account notes:

> Certain persons went into the room above the room above where they were holding services and poured water through the ceiling onto the preacher and members ... the miscreants also treated them to a pelting of raw eggs ... when they attempted to hold meetings at private homes their preacher was arrested.[58]

The local authorities decided, however, that they could no longer prosecute the "noisy" Pentecostals while doing nothing about the bars and brothels.

In 1919, when L. P. (Alverda) Griggs became the pastor, the church aligned with the Oneness group, the Pentecostal Assemblies of the World.[59] After Griggs

---

[54] See early Pentecostal responses to human trafficking in Daniel D. Isgrigg, "Rescued Women: Early Pentecostal Responses to Sex Trafficking," a paper presented at the 2021 annual meeting of the Society for Pentecostal Studies, South Lake, Texas, March 2021.

[55] "Sapulpa, Okla.," *Church of God Evangel,* June 30, 1917,

[56] *Minutes of the Thirteenth Annual Assembly of the Church of God* (1917), 59.

[57] "Notes of Praise," *Weekly Evangel,* July 10, 1915, 1.

[58] "Editorial," *Bixby Bulletin,* May 14, 1915, 14.

[59] *Minute Book of the Pentecostal Assemblies of the World 1918-1919,* Indianapolis, Indiana, Appendix A. See also *Minute Book of the Pentecostal Assemblies of the World 1919-1920,* Indianapolis, Indiana, Appendix A. There is also a mention of C. O. and Lillie Waltman of Wilmer, Oklahoma, but I found no record of that town.

and her brother, Theodore Smith, heard the Oneness message preached by G. T. Haywood in Cincinnati, they returned to lead the Apostolic Church in Skiatook and pioneer a Oneness church in Sperry.[60]

According to local UPC historian, Pastor Don Martin, in one early meeting, 77 received the baptism in the Holy Spirit and 28 were baptized in water.[61] C. P. Kilgore frequently ministered around Skiatook, Turley, and Sperry. In 1922, S. L. Ross became the pastor in Skiatook, and a church building was built.[62] Today, that church is an Assemblies of God congregation.

The work in Sperry was continued by Sister Bessie Pointer, and in 1921 a building was built for the congregation. The church was pastored by Brother Berkley, C. P. Kilgore, E. J. Hamby, and others.[63]

4.4 Skiatook Apostolic Church c. 1920

---

[60] Garrison and Westberg, *Claiming the Land*, 225.

[61] Martin, *The First Pentecostal Church of Garden City*, 27.

[62] Morris E. Golder, *History of the Pentecostal Assemblies of the World* (Indianapolis, IN: Morris E. Golder, 1973), 73.

[63] Garrison and Westberg, *Claiming the Land*, 227.

5

TULSA'S RACE MASSACRE AND THE PENTECOSTAL SURVIVORS

Tulsa's Forgotten History

No telling of Tulsa's history is complete without addressing the events of May 31–June 1, 1921. Known as the Tulsa Race Massacre, the infamous race "riot" was one of the worst acts of racial violence in American history. Yet, for generations it has been largely unknown to Tulsa residents. In a twenty-four-hour period, the all-black community along Greenwood Avenue was transformed from a thriving black community to a smoldering thirty-five square block war zone. It didn't matter if one was rich or poor, Christian or non-Christian, everyone in Greenwood was simply "a negro" and the target of one of the nation's greatest injustices. Over the next fifty years, the tale of those two days receded from the collective memory of Tulsa's white community. Succeeding generations of white Tulsans never learned of the tragic events. Even the Mayor of Tulsa admitted in 1996, "I was born and raised here and had never heard of the riot."[1]

The story of what happened to the black community was forgotten, and with it was forgotten the story of Tulsa's black Pentecostal churches. Though the story of Tulsa's white Pentecostal churches are fairly well known, no historian has asked what happened to the churches or the survivors of this racial violence.

---

[1] *Tulsa Race Riot: A Report by the Oklahoma Commission to Study the Tulsa Race Riot of 1921* (Tulsa, Oklahoma: Tulsa Race Riot Commission, 2001), 25. Oklahoma Historical Society, accessed December 16, 2020, https://www.okhistory.org/research/forms/freport.pdf.

Since the Race Massacre deeply affected the Black Pentecostal community it is part of the whole story of Pentecostalism in the city.

The Greenwood Community

The oil boom in Tulsa in the early 1900s brought prosperity to the young city of Tulsa. The economic opportunities also benefited African American citizens who were building their own "colored town" on the north side of the railroad tracks. Several African American entrepreneurs built churches, hotels, entertainment establishments, and other businesses in the Greenwood District, but numerous churches showcased the religious character of the community. As Scott Ellsworth notes,

> On a per capita basis, there were more churches in black Tulsa than there were in the city's white community as well as a number of Bible study groups, Christian youth organizations, and chapters of national religious societies. All told, there were more than a dozen African American churches in Tulsa at the time of the riot, including First Baptist, Vernon A.M.E., Brown's Chapel, Morning Star, Bethel Seventh Day Adventist, and Paradise Baptist, as well as Church of God, Nazarene, and Church of God in Christ congregations.[2]

Churches in the Greenwood District also benefited from the prosperity that Tulsa experienced from the oil boom. One of these was the iconic Mt. Zion Baptist Church. Began in 1909 as Second Baptist Church, Reverend R. A. Whitaker and congregation built a $92,000 impressive stone church that by 1921 was home to well over 900 members.[3] Another is the famous Vernon African Methodist Episcopal (AME) Church at 309 N. Greenwood Avenue. Founded in 1906, the church first met in Gurley Hall at 114 N. Greenwood Avenue at the edge of Deep Greenwood, the main commercial district. Over the next decade Pastor P. W. Delyle and the 200 members planned and constructed the stunning red brick building at 309 N. Greenwood Avenue, which helped the church to grow to 700 members by 1921.[4] At the heart of the Greenwood District, the church was a pillar

---

[2] *The Tulsa Race Riot: A Report by the Oklahoma Commission to Study the Tulsa Race Riot of 1921*, 42.
[3] Johnson, *Black Wallstreet*, 85-87. *The Polk-Hoffhine City Directory Co.'s Tulsa City Directory* (1921), 14.
[4] Ibid., 89-90.

of the community and often hosted community and civic events. In addition, there were all-black churches with larger congregations including African Methodist Episcopal Church (125), Colored Methodist Episcopal Church (350), and Wesley Chapel (150).[5]

The Greenwood Massacre

By 1921, the Greenwood District was one of the most successful black commercial districts in the U.S.—known to the whites as "Little Africa" and by its citizens as "Black Wall Street,"[6] but the prosperity of Greenwood caused jealousy from lower class white citizens of Tulsa. Tensions between blacks and whites in Tulsa came to a head on May 31, 1921, when a young black man was accused of assaulting a young white woman in a Tulsa hotel elevator. Incited by a headline in the *Tulsa Tribune* that read "Nab Negro," a large group of whites in Tulsa demanded authorities deliver the young man to a lynch mob. [7] Fearing that the Tulsa authorities would not protect the young man, a group of armed black men, some who had been soldiers in WWI, raced from Greenwood to defend him. Then "all Hell broke loose," as what started as a skirmish at the courthouse turned into an all-out war that moved from Downtown to the streets of Greenwood.[8]

Over the next twenty-four hours, Tulsa became the site for one of the worst acts of racial violence in American history. Whites and blacks exchanged fire in the streets. Planes dropped firebombs on businesses and homes while bullets rained down on black citizens from machine gun installments on top of Standpipe Hill. For their safety, authorities forcibly removed blacks from their community while white mobs looted and torched the Greenwood area.

---

[5] *The Polk-Hoffhine City Directory Co.'s Tulsa City Directory* (1921), 14-16.

[6] Mary E. Jones Parrish, *Events of the Tulsa Disaster: An Eye-Witness Account of the 1921 Tulsa Race Riot* (Mary E. Jones Parrish, 1923; repr., Tulsa, OK: Out on a Limb Publishing, 1998). This work contains the personal reflections of Ms. Parrish and others who witnessed the 1921 race riot.

[7] The *Tulsa Tribune* editorial, written by editor, Richard Lloyd Jones, read, "To Lynch a Negro Tonight." According to Hirsch, *Riot and Remembrance*, 81, the editorial was permanently "excised from the record" of newspaper archives. The only existing copies of that paper have the "entire editorial page cut out."

[8] Mary E. Jones Parish, *Events of the Tulsa Disaster:*), 8: Hirsch, *Riot and Remembrance*, 79.

5.1 Greenwood on Fire

By the end of the day, an estimated 200-250 people were killed (an estimated 80 percent were black), thousands of Tulsa's black citizens were left homeless as 35 blocks were burnt to the ground.[9] The official counts from the December 30, 1921 Red Cross report estimated 1,256 houses were burned, 215 houses were looted, and 314 were robbed.[10] The total property loss was estimated to be over $1.8 million. James Hirsh comments, "The ruins of Greenwood were a grim display of racial hatred… The riot was not only an expression of hostility between two groups but also a reflection of the isolation and mistrust each community felt for each other."[11]

Churches were among the institutions affected by the destruction. The Red Cross notes eight black churches, including one large brick building, two basement brick buildings, four one-room frame buildings, were destroyed or damaged.[12] The

---

[9] Hirsch, *Riot and Remembrance*, 118-19, notes that reports on the number of dead varied, but the director of the Red Cross estimated that the number killed could be "as high as 300." A detailed list of property losses is listed in Jones Parish, *Events of the Tulsa Disaster*, 98-112.

[10] Larry O'Dell, "Riot Property Loss," *Tulsa Race Riot: A Report by the Oklahoma Commission to Study the Tulsa Race Riot of 1921*, February 21, 2001, 144.

[11] Hirsch, *Riot and Remembrance*, 118-19.

[12] "Full Social and Medical Relief Report up to and Including December 31st, 1921," quoted in Johnson, *Black Wall Street*, 222.

destroyed include the Methodist Episcopal Church, the Colored Methodist Episcopal church, the Seventh Day Adventist Church, Paradise Baptist church, Metropolitan Baptist Church, Union Baptist Church, Mt. Zion Baptist Church and the African Methodist Episcopal Church (Vernon Chapel).[13]

For over half a century, the city, the press, and history books expunged the event from Tulsa's memory. Yet, the effects persisted in the minds of African Americans in Tulsa. In the 1970s, some of Tulsa's black community leaders brought attention to the forgotten tragedy. Three decades later, the 2001 Tulsa Race Riot Commission was formed to investigate the history and bring justice to the community. This effort garnered national attention and for the first time the city and state have recognized the incident as one of the nation's greatest acts of racial violence. Since that time, city, churches, and community organizations have worked to educate the public and begin to bring healing to the city.

As Tulsa has come to recognize the scale of this tragedy, it has changed the name of the event from the "Tulsa Race Riot" to the "Tulsa Race Massacre." The re-naming represented reclamation the original name given to it by the Greenwood community. As the official Red Cross report documents, originally different circles debated how to refer to the "riot," noting that some "unprejudiced and indirectly interested people" (i.e., the white community) referred to the event as "a riot." The report further notes that others wanted to call it "the negro uprising," but those that with "deeper feeling" about the event (i.e., the black community) "refer to it as a 'massacre'" or "the time of *dewa* (the war)." It concludes, "Whatever people choose to call it the word or phrase has not yet be coined which can adequately describe the events of June 1st." [14] That it eventually became known as the "race riot" was not accidental and was the term white Tulsans used on postcards of the burned-out community created to showcase their dominance over the Black community. With efforts for justice for the survivors, leaders have come to recognize the event's severity and call it what it was: a *massacre* of black human beings.

---

[13] Johnson, *Black Wallstreet*, 83.

[14] "Report by Maurince Williows, Tulsa County Chapter American Red Cross Disaster Relief Committee, Preface," quoted in Johnson, *Black Wall Street*, 198.

Pentecostal Survivors

One of the most challenging aspects of the story of the Pentecostal Church in Tulsa is discovering what happened to Greenwood's Pentecostal churches and believers. Did the churches survive? Did some Pentecostals die in the violence? Were their homes also destroyed? Did they leave town? The tragedy of the overall neglect of the story of black Pentecostals in Tulsa means that Pentecostal churches are missing from the list of damaged churches. This absence is not only unjust, but robs the narrative of the community's Pentecostal Church of its fullest expressions.

Although most of the survivors have since died, a few stories of Pentecostals who survived this era remain. The stories of three survivors of the Race Massacre, other stories of Tulsa residents of who lived in outside Greenwood, give us a glimpse into what black Pentecostals endured on that day. Each story provides insight into how they continued to thrive despite the devastating racial injustices of 1921.

Travis B. Sipuel (1877–1946)

T. B. Sipuel was born in Columbus, Mississippi in 1877, the son of formerly enslaved people. He was raised on a Mississippi plantation where his parents continued to work after Emancipation. Sipuel ran away at age thirteen and found various jobs in the railroads to survive. He eventually became a railroad man and soon a foreman who led teams of rail line repairmen.

5.3 Travis B. Sipuel

His wife, Martha Bell Smith, was the daughter of Cindy Smith, a female slave purchased by a white family in Tennessee. Although Martha's mother was black, Martha was fair skinned because she and her siblings were conceived by their white slave owner. [15] Travis and Martha met in McDermott, Arkansas and were married in 1908. Shortly after, they attended a revival in McDermott held by Charles H. Mason, where they were saved and heard about Pentecost. Sipuel was mentored by Mason and ordained in the Church of

---

[15] Fisher, *Matter of Black and White*, 9-10.

God in Christ. Sipuel had a brilliant mind and was a natural leader. He taught himself bookkeeping and was often called in to help churches get their finances in order.

In 1917, Bishop E. M. Page and Bishop C. H. Mason asked Sipuel and his wife to move to Tulsa to help pastor the COGIC church started in 1914. The couple found a house on North Greenwood Avenue where they could raise a family. T. B. also leased a building at 700 N. Greenwood Avenue to house the church.[16] The Sipuels were impressed with the Greenwood community and its religious character—it seemed to be a promised land. Within a short time, the church grew to over 120 people.

When the horrific violence broke out on May 31, 1921, the Sipuels were not immune. A mob of white looters invaded their neighborhood and reached their home. They stood helplessly as the men looted their possessions and set their beautiful home on fire. Meanwhile, deputized militias of white men forced Travis, along with thousands of other African American men, to march with hands held high to an internment camp at McNulty Park, Tulsa's ballpark. Meanwhile, Martha was left alone and helpless, watching their dream house burn to the ground. Because of her light complexion, one of the white militia men mistook her for being white and told her, "You better get yourself back to the white part of town before the n_s get ahold of you."[17] Sipuel spent a week in the concentration camp until finally he was allowed to leave.

---

[16] Ibid., 10.
[17] Ibid., 12.

5.4 "Captured Negros" White Supremacist Postcard

Though the Sipuels survived the Race Massacre, they lost everything and decided to leave town. They chose to settle in Chickasha, Oklahoma where they pioneered a COGIC church, and in a couple of years the church was thriving. Unfortunately, Chickasha did not prove to be a place of escape from racial violence.

On May 31st, 1930, nine years to the day after the Tulsa Race Massacre, another young black man named Henry Argo was arrested, having been accused by the white sheriff of killing a white woman. In Oklahoma's last recorded lynching, a white mob broke into the jail and shot the young man in the head. After surviving two racial incidents, Martha became active in the local NAACP chapter. Meanwhile her husband continued to pastor the Church of God in Christ and his leadership skills led Mason to appoint him as the Southwestern Oklahoma District Overseer in 1930 and State Bishop for all of Oklahoma in 1935.

While Sipuel was a significant leader in the Pentecostal community, his daughter, Ada Lois, became a national civil rights hero. After losing their firstborn, Samuel, shortly after they were married, Travis and Martha had asked Mason to pray for them to have a child. Eventually they had three children: Lemuel, Hellen Marie, and Ada Lois. Born in 1924, Ada Lois was a brilliant young woman. After excelling in High School, she received a scholarship to Arkansas A&M University, an historically black institution in Pine Bluff. When she returned home, she married Warren Fisher in 1944.

In 1945, the NAACP asked the Sipuel family about the possibility of one of their children applying to the University of Oklahoma law school in order to challenge its all white student policy. Ada Lois Fisher volunteered and on April 6, 1946, applied for admission. She was deemed academically qualified but her application was denied because, by Oklahoma law, black people were prohibited from attending the school.[18] NAACP lawyer Thurgood Marshall took her case to the Supreme Court. The court forced University of Oklahoma to create a "separate but equal" all black law school at Langston University. But this would not do for Ada Lois who wanted the same access to education and professors as white students.

5.5 Ada Lois Sipuel (Wiki)

She returned to the Supreme Court to challenge the "separate but equal" laws entrenched in Jim Crow Oklahoma, arguing that her education was not equal. The Court agreed, and her case paved the way for the *Brown vs. Board of Education* decision that would desegregate schools.[19] Finally, in June 1949, Ada Lois became a University of Oklahoma Law School student. Yet as a student she endured the humiliation of segregated seating. Upon graduating in 1952, she joined the Langston University faculty.

Ada Lois Sipuel Fisher's Pentecostal faith strengthened her resolve as a civil rights pioneer. All along, the COGIC community supported her financially and with prayers.[20] In 1992, she was appointed to the OU Board of Regents, and a garden was named in her honor. Her father died in 1946, the same year her case against OU began. Her Mother, Martha, died in 1971.[21]

The *Brown vs. Board of Education* case may not have happened had it not been for the courage of a young Pentecostal woman whose family was impacted by the

---

[18] Melvin C. Hall, "Fisher, Ada Lois Sipuel," *The Encyclopedia of Oklahoma History and Culture*, accessed December 8, 2020, https://www.okhistory.org/publications/enc/entry.php?entry=FI009.

[19] Cheryl Elizabeth Brown Wattley, *A Step toward Brown V. Board of Education: Ada Lois Sipuel Fisher and Her Fight to End Segregation* (Norman, OK: University of Oklahoma Press, 2018).

[20] Fisher, *Matter of Black and White*, 94.

[21] "Homegoing of Mother M. B. Sipuel," *The Whole Truth* 5, no. 7 (August 1971): 8.

Massacre. So, while the Massacre sought to keep blacks marginalized, God used the offspring of a survivor to forever change the racial laws of Oklahoma and the United States.

Eldoris Mae McCondiche (1911–2010)

The story of Eldoris Mae McCondiche gives greater insight into the lives of ordinary Pentecostals who stayed in Tulsa following the Greenwood tragedy. Her parents, Howard and Agusta Ector, came to Tulsa in 1915 when she was four years old. McCondichie was nine years old when she was awakened by her mother to the sound of gunfire. As they left their house and fled north, she recalls, "Bullets were coming down around us, the planes were up in the air shooting down and I could hear those bullets falling."[22] In terror, she broke away from her parents and hid in a chicken coop. Her parents knew that if they stayed, they would be killed. So, they picked her up and carried her up the railroad tracks several miles to Turley. There, a kind white family gave them food and allowed them to stay for the night in an empty home.

The next morning the family returned to the aftermath of the violence and destruction. As the train approached, they were relieved to see their house still standing on the 1400 block of North Greenwood Avenue. It had been spared because rioters thought it was in the white neighborhood. The First Baptist Church, just two blocks north, was also saved because rioters mistook it for a white church.[23] Other churches were not so lucky. McCondichie recalls, "Every church or school house that I saw were blown up."[24] The homes of teachers and doctors as well as businesses were the most targeted by the white mobs.

McCondichie's recalls that her family were members of the "Church of God and [*sic*] Christ." As they returned, she remembers her parent's delight to see that their church was still standing. This was not because the rioters did not try to

---

[22] Interview with Eldoris Mae McCondiche, Tape 3 transcript, Tulsa Race Riot Survivor Stories Collection, May 14, 1999, Oklahoma Historical Society.

[23] Johnson, *Black Wall Street*, 92.

[24] Interview with Eldoris Mae McCondiche, Tape 4 transcript, Tulsa Race Riot Survivor Stories Collection, May 14, 1999, Oklahoma Historical Society.

destroy it. She recalls that when the mob tried to burn the building they were unsuccessful. She explains, "I don't know how many times, but each time they set it afire… it wouldn't burn. The blaze would go up and then come down. So then they decided to use gasoline… the blaze would go up and go down."[25]

5.6 View from the Tulsa Pressed Brick Plant hill

McCondichie believed that God had protected that church through the prayers of the Spirit-filled members, commenting, "I knew that was God keeping us, and how hard the people worked in those days to save the church and a lot of prayer was used. And he saved that church."[26] She and her family stayed in Tulsa and helped rebuild Greenwood. Her father and grandfather were both carpenters who helped to rebuild homes and businesses. McCondichie lived the rest of her life in Tulsa. She never considered leaving because it was just "home." She told her story in several interviews of survivors before she passed away in 2010.

---

[25] ibid.
[26] ibid.

Otis G. Clark (1903–2012)

Otis Grandville Clark was among the longest living survivors of the Massacre. Clark was born in Meridian, Oklahoma Territory, in 1903 to Henry Clark and Effie Moore.[27] Soon after his birth, his father left Effie and went to work for the railroad and Effie and her son boarded a train to Tulsa to live with her parents, Aaron and Ellen Clark.

The Clarks heard that Tulsa could be a paradise for black Americans and came to Tulsa in the earliest days of Indian Territory because of the opportunities to own land and be free. Over the next few years, the city developed as a true bright spot for African Americans, particularly in Greenwood area. In 1913, Clark was one of the first Tulsans to attend the new Booker T. Washington School. At fifteen, he got a

5.7 Otis G. Clark, c 1921

job at Shackles Drug Store, delivering medicine to people suffering from the 1918 Spanish Flu epidemic.[28] Somehow, he avoided being infected himself, enjoying good health throughout his life. Many other parts of his life were not so healthy; the unchurched teenager learned to make corn whiskey from his uncle and became a notable bootlegger.

The events of 1921 changed everything for Clark. When the shooting began, Clark was hanging out on Greenwood Avenue with a friend whose father ran the Jackson Funeral Home. Clark and Jackson jumped into the funeral hearse to rescue people when Jackson was shot in the hand. Clark took off north on Greenwood Avenue and ran home to his grandparent's house. They all jumped into the car and headed out toward Claremore to escape the violence. As they returned the next day, the National Guard was there to re-establish order, but Clark's grandparent's house had been burned to the ground, and his bulldog perished inside.[29] Even worse, his mother's new husband, Tom Bryant, was never found and was presumed dead. The family never found out what happened to him. Clark's mother,

---

[27] Gweneth Williams and Star Williams, *His Story, History, and His Secret: Life through the Eyes of Otis Grandville Clark* (Tulsa: Life Enrichment Publishing, 2018), 37.
[28] ibid., 43.
[29] ibid., 52.

grandparents, and siblings moved in with his sister, Bertha, until the Salvation Army built a one-room temporary home for them a few weeks later. With five people all living in one small home, Clark left town to look for his father in Los Angeles.

In Los Angeles, Clark lived an exciting life. After holding a few hotel jobs, he became the butler and driver for Hollywood star, Joan Crawford. Through her, he met Charlie Chaplin, Clark Gable, and other Hollywood stars. But Clark continued his bootlegging and after being arrested and imprisoned heard the gospel through the ministry of the Salvation Army and gave his life to Christ. After his released, he met Emma Cotton, an Azusa Street Mission participant. By this time, William Seymour had died, and Cotton opened the Azusa Pentecostal Temple, which became a prominent early COGIC churches.[30] Cotton took Clark into her home and mentored him as he traveled with her and her husband, Henry, to her preaching engagements. With the old Azusa Mission no longer in use, a Bishop Driscol gave Clark power of attorney over it with hopes he could revive it. Ultimately, though, it failed and was closed and sold.[31] Clark was ordained by Samuel M. Crouch in Los Angeles and began to travel as an evangelist.

Clark was a global evangelist, who made his final mission trips to Africa at age 103 and the West Indies at 107 years old. He devoted the last years of his life to recounting his story as a Massacre survivor, and, in 2005, traveled with other survivors to the Supreme Court restitution hearing for survivors. Clark used these opportunities to share his message of reconciliation because he believed that the baptism in the Holy Spirit was a baptism of love that turns people into instruments of forgiveness. He was in perfect health until his death in 2012.

Mother Mattie McCaulley

Mattie McCaulley, the first female missionary commissioned by the Church of God in Christ, was a notable survivor of the Massacre. Though details of her life are scarce, we know she was in Tulsa during these years but left the city in 1926 to

---

[30] "Cotton, Emma," in *Dictionary of Pan-African Pentecostalism*, vol. 1, ed. Estrelda Y. Alexander (Eugene, OR: Wipf & Stock, 2019), 121-22.

[31] "Clark, Otis G.," Alexander, *Dictionary of Pan-African Pentecostalism*, vol. 1, 113-14.

plant churches in Trinidad.³² She and several other ministers established churches in Costa Rica and Panama.³³ McCaulley later became the supervisor for COGIC missions work throughout the region.

Mattie Carter McGlothen

One of the most influential women in the Church of God in Christ in Tulsa was Dr. Mattie Carter McGlothen. Though not resident in Greenwood in 1921, her story is worth including since she lived in nearby Sapulpa during that era. McGlothen was born in Dallas, but her parents, Evins and Crecy Carter, moved to Sapulpa right after she was born around 1904.³⁴ She attended Sapulpa Public Schools and she graduated from Quindaro College, in Kansas City, Kansas in 1922.

5.8 Dr. Mattie Carter McGlothen (McGlothen Library and Museum)

In 1921, Mattie was saved, filled with the Holy Ghost and healed of tuberculosis in a Pentecostal revival in Sapulpa's COGIC church. ³⁵ In 1923, she married Bishop George McGlothen and together they founded a COGIC church in Tulsa in the late-1920s as well as churches in Sawyer, Hugo, and Idabel.³⁶ She later served as the Women's Department Supervisor in California for sixty-one years and became the 4th General Supervisor of the International Department of Women from 1967–1994.

---

³² Glenda Williams Goodson, *Royalty Unveiled: Women Trailblazers in the Church of God in Christ International Missions, 1920-1970* (Lancaster, TX: HCM Publishing, 2011), 78-79.

³³ *Yearbook of the Church of God in Christ (1926)*, 61.

³⁴ Sherry Sherrod DuPree, "McGlothen, Mattie Carter," *Biographical Dictionary of African-American, Holiness-Pentecostals (1880-1990)* (Washington, DC: Middle Atlantic Regional Press, 1989), 184-85. See also Nancy A. Lashawn Deville, "Brief Biography of Dr. Mattie McGlothen," *Church of God in Christ, Inc. 39th Annual Women's International Convention*, Portland, OR, May 16-21, 1989, 6.

³⁵ Dr. Mattie McGlothen Library Museum, https://mcglothenlibrarymuseum.org/bio.html (accessed 7 March 2021).

³⁶ It is unclear which church was started by the McGlothlens in Tulsa as mentioned in her bios, but the *Yearbook of the Church of God in Christ (1926)*, 135, mentions the churches they pastored in Hugo and Idabell.

McGlothen founded, organized or reorganized numerous COGIC auxiliaries including the International Hospitality Department, the Education and Scholarship Fund, the Bishop's Wives Scholarship Fund, the Screening Committee for Jurisdictional Supervisors, the McGlothen Foundation, the Emergency Relief Fund, the Lavender Ladies, the Leadership Conference for Jurisdictional Leaders and National Workers, and Business and Professional Women's Federation.[37] She passed away in 1994.

Mary J. (Patterson) Hopkins

Another important COGIC survivor, Mother Mary Jane Hopkins, was born March 7, 1887 in Fayetteville, Texas. At fifteen years old she was saved and received the baptism in the Holy Spirit. Patterson married Pike Hopkins on March 23, 1912 and shortly they settled in Tulsa; some of the earliest known black Pentecostals. After the massacre, the couple moved to Detroit, Michigan where Pike joined the Police Department. He served until his death in 1939.

Mother Hopkins later became involved in COGIC Women's Department leadership, establishing churches in Texas and Michigan.[38] In 1964, she was appointed Supervisor of the Northeast Michigan Women's Department, where she served for many years and became known as "Amen Mother" for her anointed preaching and Bible teaching.[39] In 1973, Hopkins founded the United Sisters of Charity, a benevolence ministry serving Detroit, Michigan. Mother Hopkins lived to be 108 years old.

---

[37] "Mother Mattie McGlothen," Church of God in Christ, accessed December 2, 2020, https://www.cogic.org/womensdepartment/about-us/former-general-supervisors/mother-mattie-mcglothen/.

[38] "Michigan Woman, 108, Dies," UPI.com, August 7, 1995, accessed December 2, 2020, https://www.upi.com/Archives/1995/08/07/Michigan-woman-108-dies/9042807768000/.

[39] *Church of God in Christ 50th Women's International Convention* (Los Angeles, CA: Church of God in Christ, 2000), 418. USC Libraries, accessed December 21, 2020, http://digitallibrary.usc.edu/cdm/compoundobject/collection/p15799coll14/id/115744/rec/41.

White Pentecostal Silence

In over one hundred years of telling the Pentecostal story, no white historical account mentions the Massacre. As was generally the case, white Pentecostals simply did not acknowledge what had happened to their black Pentecostal brothers and sisters and often shared the cultural attitudes about blacks in Tulsa in that era. While African Americans saw Tulsa's Greenwood as "The Promised Land," whites had a completely different view. The local white press repeatedly published rumor and bigoted stereotypes that painted Greenwood as a land of vice and unruliness.[40] Reports in the *Tulsa Tribune* published a regular police blotter of arrests and rumors about the community's supposed lawlessness.[41]

These racist characterizations resulted in the excessive use of violence toward black men during the Massacre. Rather than deal with the white men who were destroying Greenwood, the National Guard rounded up over 6,000 black men and marched them with hands up to detention camps for a week under the guise of "protecting them." After the Massacre, the *Tribune* recommended that the Greenwood community not be rebuilt because it was a "cesspool of iniquity and corruption." The editorial goes on to say, "In this old 'N_ town' were a lot of badn s and a bad n is about the lowest thing that walks on two feet."[42]

The Grand Jury concluded that the Tulsa "riot" took place because of the "agitation of the negro" due to their belief "in equal rights, social equality and their ability to demand the same." [43] As Chris Messer and Patricia Bell point out, "[a]mple evidence suggests, once again, that the community was considered to be the problem, rather than a victim."[44] Even the white pastors of the Ministerial Alliance stated that the destruction was "provoked by the bad element of the

---

[40] Chris M. Messer and Patricia A. Bell, "Mass Media and the Governmental Framing of Riots: The Case of Tulsa, 1921," *Journal of Black Studies* 40, no. 5 (May 2010): 851-70.

[41] R. Halliburton, Jr., *The Tulsa Race War of 1921* (San Francisco: R and E Research Associates, 1975), 38-41.

[42] Johnson, *Black Wallstreet*, 81.

[43] Appendix I: Grand Jury Report," in R. Halliburton, Jr., *The Tulsa Race War of 1921*, 38-39.

[44] Messer and Bell, "Mass Media and the Governmental Framing of Riots," 862.

negros."[45] The insurance companies used the "riot clause" to deny claims because the mayor deemed the destruction was the "negro's fault."[46]

Framing the Massacre as an issue of upholding "law and order" in the black community bolstered beliefs by white Pentecostals that Greenwood's destruction was the community's fault. But African American leaders knew that this was not about "law and order." Rather, it was white supremacy on full display, as the editor of the *Black Dispatch*, Roscoe Dunjee, commenting days after the massacre:

> Stripped of all excuses that may be thrown around it, Tulsa's shame can be summed up in the last words of Thursday's editorial of the Oklahoman... 'THIS IS WHITE MAN'S COUNTRY.' It was the job of certain white people in Tulsa to thrust this fiat down the throats of Tulsa's black population that has caused this to happen.[47]

At the end, "Tulsa's shame" was about white dominance over a prosperous black community.

White Pentecostals around the country demonstrated the same racist attitudes toward the riots in that era. A 1917 issue of the *Pentecostal Evangel*, for example, called riots around the nation "signs of the times." In particular, it pointed to the "armed negro invasion" of East St. Louis in July of that year.[48] However, like Tulsa, the St. Louis riot, which black papers called "The Massacre of East St. Louis," was white violence against blacks that resulted in forty blacks being killed or lynched and four thousand displaced from their homes.[49] Yet, these characterizations were intended to shape public perception of African Americans and white Pentecostals chose to identify with the prejudiced culture over the plight of their brothers and sisters.

Perhaps the biggest hindrance to racial empathy with Tulsa's black Pentecostal Church was, simply, unfamiliarity. White Tulsa Pentecostals were satisfied with the

---

[45] "Statement of the Pastors of the City of Tulsa," in Johnson, *Black Wallstreet*, 196-97.

[46] Johnson, *Black Wall Street*, 99; "Tulsa City Commission Meeting Minutes, June 14, 1921," in Johnson, *Black Wall Street*, 238-39.

[47] Roscoe Dunjee, "A White Man's Country," *The Black Dispatch*, June 3, 1921, 2.

[48] J. R. Flower, "Living in Momentous Days," *Pentecostal Evangel*, July 14, 1917, 8.

[49] Alison Keys, "East St. Louis Race Riot Left Dozens Dead and Devastating a Community on the Rise," *Smithsonian Magazine*, June 20, 1917, accessed July 5, 2020, https://www.smithsonianmag.com/smithsonian-institution/east-st-louis-race-riot-left-dozens-dead-devastating-community-on-the-rise-180963885/.

racial divide. Unlike the birth of Pentecostalism at Azusa where racial mixing was intentional, white Pentecostals in Tulsa enjoyed the privilege of self-sufficiency and were content not to "cross the tracks" to fellowship with fellow Pentecostal believers. As Scott Ellsworth comments, "the vast majority of white Tulsans possessed almost no direct knowledge of the African American community whatsoever."[50] They neither knew their African American brothers and sisters, nor empathized with their plight.

What was worse is that, Pentecostalism could have been God's answer to Jim Crowism. When the outpouring of the Holy Spirit came at Azusa, many believed God was washing away the color lines caused by slavery and Jim Crow. Black leaders, such as William Seymour, C. H. Mason and G. T. Haywood were willing to integrate their denominations.

But white Pentecostals did not catch that vision and it wasn't until after the massacre that the Tulsa Ministerial Alliance invited black clergy to join.[51] As Pentecostal Assemblies of the World historian and bishop, Morris Golder, commented,

> If the White Pentecostal brethren would have stood firm against prejudice and racial injustice, having the most powerful authority (the Holy Spirit) and the most powerful message (The Gospel of Jesus Christ), they could have been the instruments of God for the destruction of this hideous ideology. But instead of fighting it, they submitted to its influence and have been affected by it even until now.[52]

As Golder mentions, white Pentecostals could have used their prophetic voice to speak out about Jim Crow attitudes, instead they adopted the cultural norm of "separate but equal," and chose silence reverting to the instilled the mindset that "They have their churches, and we have ours."

This separation is illustrated perfectly in the State Pentecostal Encampment in Tulsa in 1914. Just below a story in the August 5th *Tulsa World* about the closing of the meeting was a notice of 5,000 African Americans from Tulsa and the

---

[50] Scott Ellsworth, "The Tulsa Race Riot," *Tulsa Race Riot: A Report by the Oklahoma Commission to Study the Tulsa Race Riot of 1921*, February 21, 2001, 49.

[51] "Statement of the Pastors of the City of Tulsa," quoted in Johnson, *Black Wallstreet*, 196-97.

[52] Morris E. Golder, *History of the Pentecostal Assemblies of the World* (Indianapolis, IN: Pentecostal Assemblies of the World, 1973), 80

surrounding cities celebrating Emancipation Day in the same space vacated by white Pentecostals earlier that day. [53] One must wonder if any white Pentecostals stayed and celebrated with their black brothers and sisters? Unfortunately the answer is probably not. Instead, white Pentecostals headed home on trains and left blacks to celebrate alone.

The tragedy of 1921 took place in a time when the Pentecostal Church was thriving—yet white Pentecostals were silent. Despite their shared identity, white Pentecostals did not identify with the plight of their black brothers and sisters. This pattern has been repeated in Tulsa and in American culture in general. Perhaps, these survivors' stories will provide new ways for white Pentecostals to engage in the hard conversations about Tulsa's racial past, as well as the church's role in its injustices.

---

[53] "Negros had Celebration," *Tulsa Daily World*, August 5, 1914, 4.

6

REVIVAL IN GREENWOOD

The Race Massacre had devastating effects on the community of Greenwood. Yet, despite terrible destruction and horrific treatment by white Tulsans, many African Americans were determined to rebuild their promised land in Tulsa. Hannibal Johnson notes, "The Riot, for all its horrors, triggered a regeneration—a phenomenal display of courage and character—among Tulsa's beleaguered African-American citizens."[1] Many of the pioneers of this prosperous community believed in Tulsa and showcased their courage by rebuilding businesses. The families who stayed turned their temporary Red Cross shacks into permanent homes. Within a year, the community became a bustling economic center once again. Shops returned. Hotels were rebuilt. Business professionals and doctors re-established their offices, and new entertainment establishments revived the community. In fact, Booker T. Washington's well-known label of "Black Wall Street" was given to Greenwood after it was rebuilt. For the next twenty years, Greenwood once again thrived as a black economic center.

As Hannibal Johnson points out, one of the keys to the resiliency of the black community was the black Church. He says, "One institution has consistently steeled African-Americans against the eternal forces of oppression and the internal pressures of self-doubt: The African-American church."[2] After the tragedy, each African American church raised money and rebuilt bigger and better buildings. These churches experienced growth with some doubling in size from 1921–1925. The great success of today's Greenwood churches is largely due to the renaissance

---

[1] Johnson, *Black Wall Street*, 80.
[2] ibid., 82.

achieved out of the calamity. Pentecostals in Greenwood not only survived, but thrived. The grit and determination of these believers helped create a new era of revival in Tulsa's black Pentecostal churches.

North Greenwood/First Church of God in Christ

When Travis and Martha Sipuel lost everything in the Massacre, they made a fresh start in the Southeastern Oklahoma town of Chickasha. But there is some mystery surrounding exactly what happened to the church on North Greenwood. According to a former Tulsa District Superintendent, there are stories that the church building did not survive the Race Massacre.[3] The church had been located in the heart of the devastation but found a new site several blocks north at 1249 N. Greenwood Avenue.

However, as we saw in the testimony of survivor, Eldoris McCondichie, the building at 700 N. Greenwood Avenue may have miraculously survived an attempted arson of the church building. McCondichie's first-hand testimony certainly has tremendous weight. This is corroborated by the fact that it is not listed among the list of churches that were burned in the rioting. In addition, according to Pastor Donna Jackson of the Faith Still Standing project, the original First Church of God in Christ building remained on the hill even after the congregation moved north to the new building on the 1400 block of Greenwood.[4] This is further confirmed by the 1922 and 1923 city directories that continued to list the church at 700 N. Greenwood Avenue.[5]

Either way, Tulsa's first black Pentecostal church continued and experienced growth after the Massacre. Under Sipuel, the church grew to 140 members. As the

---

[3] Bishop L. V. Broom, interview by author, Tulsa, Oklahoma, December 4, 2020.

[4] Pastor Donna Jackson of New Beginnings Christian Church will present her presentation during "Faith Still Standing" event during the Race Massacre Centennial in May 2021. Among the churches that survived in her account is 1st Church of God in Christ, a fact that is affirmed by the Mrs. Ellene Palmer, the wife of former Superintendent E. J. Palmer.

[5] The 1923 *Polk City Directory* actually puts the church's location at 536 E. Independence, which is basically the same location, only facing Independence, rather Greenwood, explaining the different address.

congregation rebuilt in 1922, the church had grown to 250.[6] In the midst of the devastation and hatred they experienced, they turned to their faith in God and to the Church. By 1925, First Church of God in Christ was in the hands of Elder William G. Strassner. He and his wife, Eliza, and children, Roosevelt, Howard, Roy, and Lucille, lived in a home near the church at 1415 N. Greenwood Avenue.[7] In 1925, he led the Sand Springs COGIC church with J. A. Jones serving as assistant pastor and the help of Luke Davison, E. Franton, and Brother Nicholson.[8]

Strassner also served as the Overseer for Tulsa district churches. His tenure as pastor ended in 1928 when a dispute arose that brought him and the church into District Court.[9] Interestingly, the judge assigned B. C. Franklin, the prominent Tulsa lawyer, to arbitrate the case.[10] The story made national news as it was the first time an African American was appointed as "master in chancery" South of the Mason Dixon line.

Strassner's extended family is an example of the well-educated African Americans who lived in Tulsa during this time. One relative who lived next door, William R. Strassner (likely his brother), was educated at Virginia Union University in Richmond and graduated with a Bachelors of Divinity in 1922.[11] The Baptist preacher eventually became Dean of Religion at Shaw University.[12] When he left Shaw, he asked Dr. Martin Luther King, Jr. to succeed him as Dean, an opportunity

---

[6] *Polk Hoffine's Directory Co.'s Tulsa City Directory* (1922), 16. The COGIC church that was supposedly at 211 E. Independence was led by Pastor Allen Burgess and had 125 members in 1922, but there is no record of Burgesses in COGIC ministerial lists during that era.

[7] "William G Strassner in the 1940 Census," Ancestry.com, accessed December 16, 2020, https://www.ancestry.com/1940-census/usa/Oklahoma/William-G-Strassner_317zch.

[8] *Yearbook of the Church of God in Christ (1926)*, 135. Other ministers in Tulsa include Elder E. H. Augusta, R. Booker, J. H. Hawkins, Andy Murkray, Connally W. Ayers, Brother Cranshaw Modest, E. A. West, L. T. Wilson, Mose Griffins, Evangelist Anna Caldwell of Sapulpa, and Evangelist M. J. Elijah of Tulsa.

[9] One member of 1st Church recalls that after a church split, some remained in the "church on the hill" below the Brick Plant on Greenwood when the church at 1400 block was built. This mediation may have been the cause of this church split.

[10] John Hope Franklin and John Whittington Franklin, *My Life and An Era: The Autobiography of Buck Colbert Franklin* (Baton Rouge, LA: Louisiana State University Press, 1997), 222-23.

[11] *Annual Catalogue of Virginia Union University*, (1921-1922), 59.

[12] "Inaugural Address, William Russell Strassner," *Shaw University Bulletin* 21, no. 3 (November 1951): 16-22. Excerpted from DigitalNC (The North Carolina Digital Heritage Center), accessed December 6, 2020, https://lib.digitalnc.org/record/32504.

he declined.[13] Another relative, Dr. Howard Strassner Jr., of Chicago (possibly his grandson), is a 1966 Booker T. Washington High School graduate and a noted authority in obstetrics.[14]

Greater Lansing Church of God in Christ

In response to the migration of black families to homes east of the railroad tracks and the growth of COGIC believers after 1921, a new church was started in 1923. Just a few blocks east of Greenwood Avenue, Elder Charles Lincoln Lindsay and fifteen members founded a church on the 1400 block of N. Kenosha. In a short time they were able to purchase a property at 1202 N. Lansing owned by Lenna Harper. The wood-framed building had no windows and needed tar paper on the outside to keep the cold winter out. Larita Borens, the church's historian, notes that despite these humble conditions, "the Lord blessed and poured out His Spirit on these faithful pioneers and many souls were added to the church."[15]

Lindsay served for two years before leaving to pastor in Vian and was succeeded by F. M. Campbell who had been pastoring in Beggs. In 1929, Bishop Page sent A. L. Hearne and his wife, Jennie to take the pastorate. In 1930, the church experienced tremendous growth as many souls were saved during revivals conducted by outstanding ministers and missionaries. It boasted a music department with members who sang in the 1,000-voice citywide choir under the auspices of Mother Hearne. Elder Hearne also served as the Bishop of the Northeast Oklahoma COGIC.

---

[13] From Claybourn Carson, Ralph Luker, Penny A. Russell, and Peter Holloran, eds., *Rediscovering Precious Values*, vol. II of *The Papers of Marin Luther King, Jr.* (Berkeley: University of California Press, 1994), 159-60. Excerpted from Stanford University (The Martin Luther King, Jr. Research and Education Institute), accessed December 16, 2020, https://kinginstitute.stanford.edu/king-papers/documents/william-r-strassner.

[14] Ginnie Graham, "Washington High to Honor Alums," *Tulsa World*, December 3, 1998, accessed November 5, 2020, https://tulsaworld.com/archive/washington-high-to-honor-alumni/article_e873e00e-28e7-5d36-96a8-e4ad72028591.html.

[15] The history of Greater Lansing is adapted from their history posted on the website written by Larita Borens. The history was used with permission with profound gratefulness. "History of Greater Lansing Church of God in Christ," Greater Lansing COGIC, accessed August 27, 2020, https://www.greaterlansingcogic.org/history.

The church offered a Sunday school, youth programs, Sewing Circle, Home and Foreign Missions, Bible Bands, and Pastor's Aide. In 1931, the congregation outgrew to the capacity of the old building. Elder Hearne and some of the men of the church tore down the old building and built an A-frame building with windows and doors. The congregation continued to grow, and in 1946, God gave the vision to rename the church Lansing Street Church of God In Christ. As the church continued to prosper financially, the elders remodeled the building and added stone to the outside. This made a beautiful place of worship and an asset to the community.

Historic Buford Colony

One consequence of the Race Massacre was the flight of some black residents to safer communities, including the Buford Colony near Prattville/Sand Springs.[16] The area was named for John Buford, a cotton farmer who gave land to his black sharecroppers. Buford had been a successful member of the community, serving as an art teacher and football coach at Booker T. Washington High School in Sand Springs. From the small group of homes they built in 1907, the community eventually grew to become an established all-black neighborhood with churches and entertainment establishments. The all-black community was small and primitive, having no utilities until the 1940s.

One church established in Buford Colony was founded by a COGIC group who settled in the colony.[17] After the Massacre, the first building built was a small open-air tabernacle that wasn't much more than a slab, four pillars, and a roof, but afforded the saints to have a place where they could sing and shout together. Several preachers came and went, but the church was held together by the women and men of the Colony. The details are few, but they later built a more permanent

---

[16] Manny Gamallo, "Cleanup to Give a Shot in the Arm to Former All-Black Buford Colony," *Tulsa World*, May 27, 1991, accessed November 20, 2020, https://tulsaworld.com/archive/cleanup-to-give-a-shot-in-arm-to-former-all-black-buford-colony/article_355c2e3b-ff57-5f45-8433-a1a469903720.html.

[17] "About," Historic Buford Colony Church of God in Christ," accessed December 16, 2020, http://www.bufordcolonycogic.org/About. The church is said to have been started as early as 1907.

church that exists today. Some of the first believers who came from Tulsa as small children have recently passed away, but have left stories of their community to the next generation.

6.1 Buford Colony Church of God in Christ (Myles Dement)

New Bethel-South Haven

Survivors of the Massacre also migrated to South Haven, a black community of West Tulsa. In 1921, as Oscar U. Schlegel sold plots from his 80-acre homestead to African Americans to rebuild. The area became a black community with churches, such as Mount Zion Baptist Church and South Haven Church of God in Christ. Many of the residents worked on the railroad in nearby Redfork and, like the Buford Colony, the community did not have basic utilities and remained fairly underdeveloped until it was annexed by Tulsa around 1960.[18]

In the 1920s, F. M. Campbell, a notable early leader in Oklahoma who was also the pastor of Beggs COGIC church, founded the South Haven congregation. There are few records about the church's history, but its members were among those who survived the Massacre. Although the

---

[18] https://www.cityoftulsa.org/media/1554/southwestp1_2.pdf

congregation did not have much, they found hope for a new life and healing in the Holy Spirit and stood as a pillar in the community. Some of the other pastors in its history are Elder A. L. Hearn, Elder Kennedy, and Elder James and Daisy Ciggs. Today New Bethel COGIC is led by Pastor Frank Brazwell.

During the 1940s, the church shared its building at 3805 W. 55th Street with Cornerstone Baptist Church while they built their building. This began a long friendship between the churches that continues today.[19]

Friendship Missionary Baptist Church

The only non-COGIC Black church in this era with Pentecostal roots is Friendship Missionary Baptist Church, most known for its most famous pastor, L. L. Tisdale. Its history goes back to 1922 when it was established by six Spirit-filled believers: Horace and Hazel Smith, Willie and Maggie Smith, and Omer and Virginia Maxville. [20] Beginning with a weekly meeting, they gathered prayer bands that sought to proclaim the gospel to Tulsa. The first pastor was H. J. Hammond, and the first services were held in a house at the 1900 block of Midland Street near Tecumseh. The church eventually moved to Lansing and Marshall Street. When Hammon passed away in 1929, he was succeeded by J. H. Russaw for a short time and Vernon B. Moore, a graduate of Morehouse College, became pastor in 1930. Moore moved the church to Queen Place and Midland. He pastored until his death in 1955 when C. J. Smith, the son of the founders, Horace and Hazel Smith, came to pastor.

In 1976, Dr. L. L. Tisdale was called to pastor the church. The "Holy Ghost Preaching and Singing Pastor" was a charismatic leader who invested in youth programs. Under his leadership, the church grew from 150 to 1000 members. On March 12, 1983, it broke ground for the present building at 1709 N. Madison

---

[19] "Greater Cornerstone Baptist Church History," Tulsa, Oklahoma, January 2018. https://irp-cdn.multiscreensite.com/8d64d8e8/files/uploaded/GCBC_History.pdf

[20] Tom McCloud and Tara Lynn Thompson, *Journey: Tulsa's Century of Christian Faith, Leadership and Influence*. (Tulsa, OK: McCloud Media, 2006), 150-51; Friendship Church history, "Church History," Friendship Church, accessed October 31, 2020, http://friendshipchurchtulsa.org/church-history/.

Avenue. L. L. Tisdale died on March 28, 1997, and the Osage Parkway in North Tulsa was named in his honor. He was followed by Pastor Weldon L. Tisdale who blended his Baptist roots with Pentecostal beliefs. He invested in a community resource center to help young people with education and life skills. Today, the church is pastored by Jamaal Dyer who has continued to strengthen the church's rich legacy of multi-generational ministry and focus on the community.

7

CENTENNIAL PENTECOSTAL CHURCHES

The 1920s was a crucial era for the growth of the Pentecostal movement in Tulsa. Several important revivals birthed a second wave of Pentecostal churches and were largely responsible for establishing a number of today's centennial churches. The first revival that helped build the Pentecostal community was the Aimee Semple McPherson revival that took place in 1918 during the global "Spanish Influenza" pandemic. The second revival was the Raymond T. Richey healing revival in 1921 where more than 10,000 people heard the Pentecostal message proclaimed and demonstrated in healing lines. These revivals were largely responsible for a second wave of believers who experienced the Holy Spirit and helped start some of Tulsa's most famous and long-standing Pentecostal churches.

Aimee Semple McPherson and the Spanish Flu Epidemic

In the middle of the 1918 "Spanish Influenza" epidemic, an up-and-coming evangelist named Aimee Semple McPherson came to Tulsa. She was invited by S. A. Jamieson, to conduct a meeting beginning November 3, 1918.[1] Jamieson and the two hundred congregants of 5th and Peoria had fasted and prayed in anticipation of her coming. She encouraged those in Tulsa to "drop all differences and non-essential issues" and attend her Pentecostal meeting where "God [would] reveal his great might and power and glory."[2] However, the sudden onset of the influenza in Tulsa prompted Jamieson to postpone the meeting since city officials

---

[1] "Announcement of Meetings," *The Bridal Call*, October 1918, 16-18.
[2] "Tulsa, Oklahoma," *Bridal Call*, November 1918, 11.

closed all public meetings. McPherson testified that the Spirit had urged her to come to Tulsa anyway and "Start immediately," so she trekked across the Midwest and arrived on Sunday November 10, 1918. She recalls, "Looking across the great stretches of prairie, the city of Tulsa came into view, and as we saw the skyline, the buildings and paved streets, after wading through the slough of despond we just shouted and praised the Lord, for it seemed as though that must be the way it will be when a soul is nearing Heaven."[3] As she arrived, she learned that the ban on church gatherings had been lifted and immediately started holding services.

> From the first meeting until she left, the Spirit's presence and power were felt, sinners were saved, seekers after the baptism received the precious gift of the Holy Ghost and many were healed. … On one night the power of God was very manifest, so much so that her hands burned like fire, and as she touched the saints, they felt the power and many were slain under the power.[4]

McPherson's ministry went beyond the walls of the church. One strategy was to drive her "Gospel Car" around town in-between meetings, stopping to minister to people on the street corners and pass out tracts. She remarks, "We found in the street work an undreamed-of wealth of opportunity for personal contact with the sinner and the down-cast."[5] Her Gospel Car was equipped with a large fold out chart illustrating the road to Heaven and the road to Hell. As many as twenty men and women at a time came to Christ on the sidewalks. In one account, two women knelt on the sidewalk and "tears splashed on the running-board." After McPherson stopped at the Tulsa Iron Works at 6th and Troost and preached to the foundry workers, some of the men came to her revival and gave their lives to Jesus.

---

[3] "Notes from the Log Kept on the Transcontinental Auto Trip Thus Far," *Bridal Call*, December 1918, 16.

[4] "A Testimony and Report from Pastor S. A. Jamieson, of Assembly of God Tabernacle, Tulsa, Okla.," *Bridal Call*, December 1918, 9-10.

[5] "Gospel Auto News," *Bridal Call*, January 1919, 10-11.

7.1 McPherson Gospel Car 1919 (HSRC)

On the streets, McPherson saw first-hand the effects the Spanish Influenza on the city. Although Tulsa was not affected as greatly as many U. S., cities, by October, it had 4,000 cases but only 28 deaths due to the halting of public gatherings, including churches.[6] McPherson notes that, "There were ceaseless calls for visiting among epidemic victims day and night."[7] She says, "The epidemic still raging, and many having been weakened and afflicted, we stood hours at a time praying for the sick, and Jesus helped those who came to him." [8] While there no specific testimonies of healing were given, one report notes, "We were called into homes where poor people were lying so low their eyes seemed glassy, and the rattle in their throats, but the Lord marvelously raised them up!"[9] Unfortunately, after her time of ministry, the city had several more waves of the influenza until April of 1919, and a total of 7,350 people died of the virus.[10]

In May of 1919, McPherson returned to Tulsa to hold another revival. This meeting was advertised regionally to Pentecostals in the surrounding states.

---

[6] "Influenza Toll Figures Higher," *Tulsa Morning World*, October 11, 1918, 1.

[7] "Gospel Auto News," *Bridal Call*, January 1919, 10-11.

[8] "Revival Meetings," *Bridal Call*, January 1919, 14-15.

[9] "Revival Meetings," *Bridal Call*, January 1919, 14-15.

[10] Debbie Jackson, "Throwback Tulsa: 1918 Flu Outbreak Brought Quarantine to Tulsa," *Tulsa World*, March 19, 2020, accessed August 9, 2020, https://tulsaworld.com/news/local/history/throwback-tulsa-1918-flu-outbreak-brought-quarantine-to-tulsa/article_9be88df8-6f23-51e5-9920-2a5f10c79eb6.html.

Anticipating a huge crowd, Jamieson secured the three thousand-seat Tulsa Convention Center. The crowds were enormous and as many as 250 people were at the altar every night. This became one of the most important meetings that built Tulsa's Pentecostal community, as over 200 were saved, and 100 received the baptism in the Holy Spirit.[11]

These two meetings not only helped the Pentecostal community grow exponentially but also helped McPherson become a household name, as a reporter dubbed her "Lady Billy Sunday."[12] When the local press questioned her right to preach as a woman, she responded, "Was she not the first to bring sin into the world? Should she not also help to redeem the world from the consequences of the fall?"[13]

7.2 1919 Pentecostal Evangel Ad

The fruit of her revivals provided a great boost to the Pentecostal Movement and paid great dividends to the exponential growth of the 5th and Peoria Tabernacle. But she also helped spread belief in healing within Tulsa's church community, as attendees heard the full gospel message, including that healing. Mrs. Tyred Berwald testified,

> The Lord worked in a mighty way, and the power fell, saving sinners, baptizing saints with the Holy Spirit. I heard the true Gospel preach and, Oh, how I praise the Dear Lord! The Holy Ghost convicted me of sin and Jesus washed me with his precious blood and baptized me with the Holy Ghost. I spoke in tongues as they did on the day of Pentecost.[14]

By using the convention center and drawing crowds in the thousands, she exposed multitudes to Pentecostal revivalism and spirituality in ways that had not

---

[11] "Tulsa Evangelistic Meeting," *The Christian Evangel*, June 14, 1919, 9; "Report of the Tulsa Evangelistic Meetings Conducted by Evangelist Aimee Semple McPherson, at Convention All," *Bridegroom's Messenger*, June 1919, 4.

[12] "How God Captured the Press," *The Latter Rain Evangel*, July 1919, 12. "Woman Initiates Revival Tonight," *Tulsa Morning Times*, May 17, 1919, 3.

[13] "Parade Precedes Revival Sermon," *Tulsa Morning Times*, May 22, 1919, 7.

[14] "Healed of Appendicitis," *Bridal Call*, February 1920, 19

yet been witnessed by mainline Christians and legitimized the Pentecostal community in Tulsa. From there a next generation of new Pentecostal churches would spring up. Despite this, congregations from her Foursquare Church did not take root in Tulsa until several decades later.[15]

Peoria and Haskell Mission/Woodlake

Inspired by McPherson's revival, Sam Berryhill opened a mission several blocks north at N. Peoria and Haskell Street. The Mission, which occupied a small house donated by the Welker Family, was later expanded to a larger building. Berryhill served three years then left to pastor West Tulsa Assembly in 1923. Over the next decade, the church was served by several pastors for short periods. Marvin Hartz came in 1936 and served the church for the next thirty years. In 1942, he built a new brick building at 705 N. Quaker, one block East of the original building and renamed the church Capitol Hill Assembly of God.

In 1966, Armon Newburn came to Capitol Hill and greatly expanded the influence of the church. By the early 1970s, Newburn had distinguished himself as one of the most notable pastors in Oklahoma. His success led him to build a new facility in a suburban area at 7100 E. 31st Street (between Sheridan and Memorial). Once again, with the move came a new name: Woodlake Assembly of God. In 1983, Newburn was elected District Superintendent of the Oklahoma District Council of the Assemblies of God where he provided leadership to the state.

---

[15] The 1936 Census of Religious Bodies records no Foursquare Gospel churches in Oklahoma. See also, "Tulsa Oklahoma," *The Foursquare Magazine*, September 1961, 9-10.

7.3 Haskell and N. Peoria Mission (Woodlake AG)

Stepping into the pastorate at Woodlake was H. A. Brummet, the former president of the Southwestern Assemblies of God University. Under Brummet, Woodlake would become one of the leading churches in the denomination in annual missions giving. He also led Woodlake to plant a church in Glenpool.[16] Brummett served for twelve years and was followed by Ted Heaston who served from 1995–2009.

In 2009, Woodlake elected Jamie Austin as the pastor. With his return to his home church, Austin's leadership led to tremendous growth. Four years earlier, property suburban Bixby had been given to the church for a future location and plans were drawn up for moving there. First, though, Austin took the Glenpool church at 14460 S. Elwood back under its wing as a new campus. In 2015, the Bixby location was opened at 10444 S. Mingo, and eventually the historic building on 31st Street was sold.

Today, Woodlake has three locations including Bixby, Glenpool, and Turley. Turley Assembly has a history that goes back to the 1920s.

---

[16] This history is adapted with gratitude to Pastor Jamie Austin from "Woodlake Assembly of God History," Woodlake Church, Bixby, Oklahoma, n.d.

Full Gospel Tabernacle/Central Assembly

As the first Pentecostal church in Tulsa, by 1914, 5th and Peoria Mission was the flagship church for Assemblies of God in Oklahoma. Several significant pastors, including W. T. Gaston and S. A. Jamieson had led the congregation. Though Gaston was an AG leader, the church did not officially join the denomination until June 4, 1917 under Jamieson. The incorporation was partly motivated by the early Pentecostal emphasis on pacifism in response to WWI. The official board meeting minutes record, "… the pastor explained the purpose of the meeting to the congregation and read a part of a bill recently passed by Congress shewing [sic] who were [sic] exempt from war." The resolution affirms,

> We as a body of Christians, while purposing to fulfill all the obligation of loyal citizenship, are nevertheless constrained to declare we cannot conscientiously participate in war and armed resistance which involved the actual destruction of human life, since it is contrary to our view of the clear teachings of the inspired word of God.[17]

This position was the primary position by the Assemblies of God and many other Pentecostal denominations.[18]

Jamieson's move to bring McPherson to Tulsa paid great dividends for the church which nearly doubled from the hundreds of converts in her meetings, but that growth would be short lived as Jamieson left in early 1920 to help the General Council to open a Bible School in Nebraska.

Harry E. Bowley (1920–1924) followed Jamison when he returned from serving as missionaries in Cape Palmas, Liberia.[19] The well-known minister was quickly recognized as a leader and chosen as Superintendent of the Oklahoma AG and as a General Presbyter.[20] During his short years, Bowley hosted annual revivals

---

[17] "Business Meeting Minutes, Full Gospel Tabernacle," May 27, 1917, Flower Pentecostal Heritage Center, Springfield, MO.

[18] Paul Alexander, *Peace to War: Shifting Allegiances in the Assemblies of God* (Telfor, PA: Cascadia Publishing House, 2009).

[19] See "General Council Department," *Pentecostal Evangel*, November 12, 1921, 8; "Tulsa, Okla.," *Pentecostal Evangel*, April 1, 1922, 9. Harry E. and Rhodema Bowley first served as missionaries in Cape Palmas, Liberia in 1916-1917 alongside John M. Perkins (not related to Jonathan E. Perkins). "Cape Palmas, Liberia," *Weekly Evangel*, July 28, 1917, 12. The Central Assembly history, "Journey Through Time," includes a full list of pastors.

[20] See "General Council Department," *Pentecostal Evangel*, November 12, 1921, 8.

that helped bring people into the Pentecostal experience. A revival in January 1922 saw seventy-five people come to Jesus, and many were baptized in the Holy Ghost.[21] During a September revival, Bowley commented, "Many new faces were at the altar night after night seeking God for the precious baptism in the Holy Spirit."[22] Bowley left for Texas in 1924.

7.4 5th and Peoria, Pastor Harry Bowley, c. 1923 (IFPHC)

Jonathan Ellsworth Perkins was another significant pastor who served at 5th and Peoria from 1924–1926. Perkins testimony shows how the Pentecostal experience can change a person's prejudice against people of color. A Methodist Episcopal pastor reared in Virginia under Scottish parents. Perkins was deeply prejudiced toward blacks.

In 1909, Perkins was invited to a Pentecostal mission in Wichita, Kansas that had both white and black members. He agreed, but when the testimony service went long, and Pentecostal spirituality took over, he became annoyed. He recalls, "One old colored Auntie got up and began to praise God and soon gave hilarious vent to her religious ecstasy." When things got even more raucous, Perkins felt bitterness and prejudice stir up in him, and he stormed out, declaring, "I was not called upon to worship God with 'n_." Back at home, he felt remorse, but

---

[21] "Tulsa, Okla.," *Pentecostal Evangel*, April 1, 1922, 9.
[22] "Tulsa, Okla.," *Pentecostal Evangel*, November 11, 1922, 20.

refused to return to apologize because he felt the leadership was wrong for not keeping "n_ where they belonged." For the next fourteen years, Perkins testified that God punished him for his prejudice by not allowing him to be exposed to Pentecost again.[23]

Finally, in 1923, while ill, Perkins read McPherson's book about Pentecost and became hungry for the baptism in the Holy Spirit and for healing. A friend invited him to a service at her Pentecostal mission on the north side of Wichita. Surprisingly, when the black pastor found out Perkins was a minister, he asked him to preach. He admitted to the congregation, "I had never been around Pentecostal folks since that colored woman scared me away." Deeply remorseful over his prejudice, he shared his need for the baptism in the Spirit.

That night, he received the fullness of the Spirit and spoke in tongues. He recalls, "I turned down the Pentecostal truth fourteen years before because of a black-skinned woman, but I had to wade through a whole campmeeting of them when I got the baptism. God surely broke me over the wheel of my prejudice."[24] Later that year, he opened a Pentecostal Mission in Wichita, Kansas, and Agnes Ozman LaBerge joined in to help him.[25] In 1924, Perkins wrote one of the first books on the baptism in the Holy Spirit by an AG pastor, *The Brooding Presence*. Perkins also served with Stanley Frodsham as Associate Editor for the *Pentecostal Evangel*.

In 1925, Perkins came to Tulsa to pastor 5th and Peoria for two years.[26] In that position, his largest accomplishment was raising $50,000 to build the brick tabernacle in August of that year. The congregation also began calling the church "Full Gospel Tabernacle." In 1926, Perkins discussed with Oklahoma ministers opening Bell Bible Institute with a literary (elementary) and high school in addition to a ministry training institute in honor of the late E. N. Bell.[27] Though the school hoped to open in the fall of 1926 with Perkins as president, Glenn

---

[23] Jonathan E. Perkins, "My First Sermon That I Did Not Preach," *The Pentecostal Evangel*, March 22, 1924, 6-7.

[24] Perkins, "My First Sermon That I Did Not Preach," 7.

[25] LaBerge the first person to speak in tongues at Charles Parham's Bethel Bible College in Topeka, Kansas. A. N. O. LaBerge, "Wichita, Kansas," *The Pentecostal Evangel*, January 5, 1924, 13.

[26] "Journey Through Time," 4; *General Council Minutes 1914-1925*, 41, 88.

[27] "Bell Bible Institute to be Opened in Tulsa, Oklahoma," *Pentecostal Evangel*, January 2, 1926, 4.

Millard as secretary, and J. W. Welch as Dean, he left before it opened. Instead, Oklahoma AG ministers placed support behind the Southwestern Bible Institute in Enid, founded by P. C. Nelson in 1927.[28]

Raymond T. Richey Revival

One of the most famous Pentecostal tent revivalists and healing ministers was Raymond T. Richey, who in 1920, launched a healing ministry in Fort Worth, TX. As word of his successful healing ministry spread and Richey grew in popularity, over the next few years, thousands came to Christ and were healed.[29]

In March 1923, the Tulsa Ministerial Alliance invited Richey to the city. Led by radio pastor, William Kitchen, the multi-denominational committee solicited funds to build a tabernacle to accommodate the crowds during the seven-week campaign.[30] The land was donated by Charles Page, and he, along with several businessmen, financed a $4,000 tabernacle to hold over 1,000 people at the northwest corner of Brady and Detroit.

Richey's revival was a huge success. The *Pentecostal Evangel* reported, "This is said by Mr. Richey and party to be the greatest revival ever held. The number of professed conversions is 10,400. 9,000 healing cards were issued."[31] The local newspapers in Tulsa were eager to cover the spectacle, and Richey's style was captured by a local reporter:

> Before them, in a white light of the platform stood a frail, white faced evangelist. His clear, magnetic voice rang out earnest confidence. The expectant sufferers raised their heads and listened intently to his prayer for them. Some said they were helped, one threw away his cane, some even claimed they were cured.[32]

---

[28] P. C. Nelson, "New Assembly and Bible School at Enid, Okla.," *Pentecostal Evangel*, June 25, 1927, 13.

[29] Glenn Gohr, "Raymond T. Richey, a Man with a Burning Message," *Assemblies of God Heritage* 22, no. 4 (Winter 2002-2003): 6-11.

[30] "Start Next Week on Tabernacle for the Richeys," *Tulsa Tribune*, March 15, 1923, 3.

[31] "Triumphs in Tulsa," *Pentecostal Evangel*, August 4, 1923, 8.

[32] "Afflicted Say Faith Healing Brings Relief," *Tulsa Tribune*, April 3, 1923, 6.

Stories about the Richey revival filled the papers, including testimonies of healings and skeptical criticisms of his claims. The publicity fueled interest in the services and spurred nightly crowds of 7,500 people.³³ The local paper estimated that 60,000 people from the area came for the revival, with an economic impact of $240,000 to the city's economy.³⁴ Page brought

7.5 1923 Tulsa World Ad

children from his children's home to experience the revival. One home for the elderly complained that so many residents were healed that its Superintendent was thinking of closing it.³⁵

With only one service of the seven-week revival open to African Americans, the black community met the opportunity with great excitement. When Richey asked, "Who wants to be healed?," he was shocked to see half of crowd raise their hands. Assisted by five black pastors, he prayed for 832 people one by one.³⁶ When the altar call was given for salvation, 759 responded to the invitation. As he laid hands on each of the attendees, there was great jumping and shouting. A reporter captured the scene:

> 'Praise the Lord,' and 'Oh, Glory, glory!' arose in screams and yells all over the building as the negroes prayed and surrendered their lives to God. Some jumped up and down, waving their arms in the air and yelling at the tops of their voices. Sing? Yes, they sang! Such singing as was never heard in that tabernacle before.³⁷

One testimony was of twelve-year-old James Baxter who was deaf, dumb, and blind. His grandmother, Virginia Spencer, brought him to the crusade from the deaf home in the all-black town of Taft. After receiving prayer, the child could both see and hear again. He spent the rest of the service picking up objects to see them. Tulsa's African Americans were not the only minority groups interested in

---

[33] "Thousands Are Turned Away at Richey Meeting," *Tulsa Tribune*, May 28, 1923, 3.
[34] "Women Holding Men from God, Richey Asserts," *Tulsa Tribune*, June 11, 1923, 10.
[35] "Richey May Empty County Poor Home," *Tulsa Tribune*, May 12, 1923, 1.
[36] "Richey Prays for 832 Negros in 63 Minutes," *Tulsa Tribune*, June 12, 1923, 12.
[37] ibid.

Richey's meetings. Native American tribal leaders invited Richey to hold a pow-wow with them so that he could minister to the members of their tribes.³⁸

One of the highlights of his Campaign was a parade through downtown Tulsa on the last Saturday night. Hundreds in the revival marched down the street led by a "donkey band" playing revival songs and a truck "piled high with discarded crutches." Some who claimed they had been healed carried their crutches or held signs declaring, "I was healed." The parade marched down Main Street to 3rd and halted traffic. The *Tulsa World* declared, "The Richey's are leaving Tulsa a better community than they found it."³⁹

The famous blind pianist, Fred Henry, was converted during a Nazarene revival. Later, he and his wife were baptized in the Holy Spirit in Tulsa. His song, "For Tulsa Jesus Died," became so popular that he changed the words to "For Sinners Jesus Died" so it could be sung anywhere.⁴⁰ Henry was a brilliant and trained musician, who, it is said, memorized over 3,000 gospel songs and could play any instrument. During Richey's revival, Henry reported having improved eyesight, but not never fully healed. Though the local skeptics often pointed to this as proof that Richey's healings were fabricated, Henry became the regular pianist at Richey's campaigns across the nation over the next decade.

In October, Richey returned to Tulsa for a second campaign, which had much less fanfare. The revival had 1,400 converts, and 1,200 claimed healing. However, Richey's revival and the tabernacle had an impact well beyond just the Pentecostal churches. Many pastors and congregants from other Protestant churches frequented the meetings in 1923. When Richey departed, the Tabernacle remained an ecumenical home for various ministers to hold their own revival meetings, including R. J. W. Able of First Methodist, W. F. Garvin of Bullette Presbyterian, and J. T. Early of the Nogales Avenue Baptist Church.⁴¹

---

³⁸ "Indians Study Coue Doctrine," *Tulsa Tribune*, March 6, 1923,

³⁹ "Triumphs in Tulsa," *Pentecostal Evangel*, August 4, 1923, 8.

⁴⁰ Glenn Gohr, "Walking by Faith, Not by Sight," *Assemblies of God Heritage* 14, no. 1 (Spring 1994): 10-13. Henry became the pianist at 5th and Peoria under Pastor Harry Bowley.

⁴¹ "Richey Tabernacle to be Available for Use of All Denominations," *Tulsa Tribune*, November 25, 1923, 10.

Faith Tabernacle Assembly of God

Faith Tabernacle in Tulsa was one of the churches deeply impacted by the Richey Revival. During the meetings, a Presbyterian minister named William Freeman Garvin became convinced that healing was for today. Garvin grew up in Ohio and attended college at Moody Bible Institute and Lane Theological Seminary. He eventually moved to Tulsa to pastor a Presbyterian mission church where he heard about the Pentecostal baptism in the Spirit, an experience he believed he had already received when he was called into ministry.[42] His growing interest in Pentecostal teachings like healing led him to attend the Richey Revival.

Convinced healing was for today, Garvin taught it in his Presbyterian church, but it was not received well. But Garvin became more involved in the revival services. Charles Page took note of Garvin and asked him to pray for his healing of diabetes. After the Richey services closed, Page allowed Garvin to continue to hold services until Page could find a buyer for the property. Page admired that Garvin would take a stand for his new Pentecostal beliefs, even to lose his congregation. Page's biographer notes, "Charles Page admired a man who let the Spirit lead him, whether it was the popular thing to do or not."[43]

Garvin continued to hold services in the large tabernacle but invited many other evangelistic parties to come minister. One such evangelist was Uldine Utley, who ministered in Faith Tabernacle October 19-November 9, 1924. [44] Utley preached the baptism in the Spirit and convinced Garvin and his wife to seek for this experience. A few days later, they both received the baptism in the Holy Spirit on November 12, 1924.[45] Several others in the small but committed congregation also received the baptism in the Spirit, including Etta Henry, wife of Fred Henry the famous blind pianist.[46]

---

[42] "History of Faith Church," Tulsa, Oklahoma, 2020.

[43] Clark, *A Fool's Enterprise*, 256.

[44] Thomas A. Robinson, *Preacher Girl: The Uldine Utley and the Industry of Revival* (Waco, TX: Baylor University Press, 2016), 122-25. Uldine Utley was a famous girl evangelist born in Durant, Oklahoma in 1912. Her parents, Azle and Hattie Utley, had settled in Lawton in the Oklahoma Territory during the land run near Lawton. It was there that the Utley's became friends with the famous Native American leader, Geronimo. During the 1920s, from age eleven until twenty-four years old, Utley became a famous Pentecostal Flapper Era "girl evangelist" in the United States.

[45] *Constitution and Bylaws of Faith Tabernacle of the Assemblies of God*, 6.

[46] Gohr, "Walking by Faith," 10-13.

In early 1925, Charles Page told Garvin that God had spoken to him about building a church for Garvin's Faith Tabernacle congregation. Page told Garvin,

> The Lord didn't call me to preach and He didn't call you to make money. But if I make the money, and you do the preaching, and I furnish the money for a church for you to preach in, that will make me a kind of preacher, won't it? You surely would not deny me the pleasure of being of a preacher in this manner?[47]

Page described to Garvin the details of the building that God showed him. It turns out that what he described was identical to what had also been given to Garvin in a dream. Page purchased a lot at 13th and Trenton for the new church.

In August 1925, they broke ground on the new brick church and held the first service December 11, 1925 with more than 100 people in attendance. Since Richey's revival was largely responsible for many of the members of the church, Garvin asked Richey to perform the dedication ceremony in June 1926. The church was officially incorporated on July 17, 1926. As the church continued to grow, space was needed for Sunday school and other church needs. In October 1928, the church purchased the frame building from the old Boston Avenue AME Church at 5th and Boston and moved it onto the property.[48] In 1940, the frame building was replaced with a more permanent building. In 1970, the church moved into a new building at 21st and Memorial, under Pastor Harry Myers.

---

[47] "History of Faith Church," Tulsa, Oklahoma, 2020.

[48] Adapted from W. F. Garvin's history of the Church in the *Constitution and Bylaws of Faith Tabernacle of the Assemblies of God*, 7-10.

7.6 Faith Tabernacle c. 1940s (Faith Church)

Although Garvin was ordained with the Assemblies of God, Faith Tabernacle remained an independent church until 1940. Some of the other pastors included Tommy Hollingsworth, L. J. Underwood, Don Mallough, Harry Myers, Grady Adcock, Bill T. Storie, Markus Alexander, and Ernest Strong. Today, the church is pastored by Dr. Kelly and Lisa Goins, who became pastors in August 2003. In 2016, a new location was chosen at 81st and Memorial and renamed Faith Church.

Pentecostal Rescue Mission

One of the other Pentecostal works that came out of the Richey Revival was the Tulsa Pentecostal Rescue Mission. Mr. and Mrs. J. P. Gallagher, owners of Bohenfeld Cleaning Works, attended the revival. Mrs. Gallagher was healed of being an invalid at the Richey meeting in 1922. Immediately they left secular work to give themselves to religious work. Mr. Gallagher said, "It is our belief that Tulsa needs a real honest-to-goodness rescue mission. ... We need a place where real down and outers will be given a chance to get on their feet."[49] The Gallaghers worked closely with the local police and courts to take charge of individuals who were "going down the wrong path." They operated their street

---

[49] "Family, Faith Healed, Plans Rescue Mission for Tulsa," *Tulsa Tribune*, September 12, 1923, 1.

ministry at First and Main Street on Thursday and Saturday Nights. The rescue mission provided food and housing, an employment agency, and spiritual training through Pentecostal ministry, but they also used their mission work to lead people to Christ and bring them into the baptism of the Holy Spirit.[50] Their work in the social ministry was thought to fill a gap that the Mission of Redeeming Love was not filling.

Carbondale/West Tulsa Assembly

The community of Carbondale is on the West Side of Tulsa, near the Red Fork area. The roots of the Pentecostal churches in the area go back at least to 1922, but probably further. West Tulsa Assembly was pastored by Brother James and in 1922 invited W. H. Whelchel to hold meetings for him. Whelchel reported, "I am having a wonderful meeting in this place. Many people getting saved and baptized with the Holy Ghost; sick are being healed. The mission will not hold all the people."[51] The revival continued throughout the year, and many people were baptized in the Spirit. In 1923, Samuel J. Berryhill became pastor and continued the revival. In April, a revival brought thirty people to Christ, and twelve received the baptism in the Holy Spirit.[52] Berryhill continued until 1924, when he was followed by Pastor W. R. Brock in 1925.[53] Brock began working on building a new church for the congregation on West 20th Street. The church was completed in November 1926. [54] Brock continued to lead the church, inviting evangelists to come regularly that help build the Pentecostal flock in West Tulsa.

In the 1930s, F. A. Hill led a mission in the community of Red Fork, which became a full gospel church and joined the Assemblies of God in September 1933. In February 1934, a small group of Pentecostal believers in Carbondale held a meeting in an upper room of the Carbondale Drug store at West 48th Street and S. 31st West Avenue. These six families were led by J. C. Minor. Pastor Phil Taylor

---

[50] Opal Sievert, "From Then Until Now," *Christ Ambassadors Monthly*, February 1930, 5.
[51] W. H. Whelchel, "West Tulsa, Okla.," *Pentecostal Evangel*, March 18, 1922, 22.
[52] S. J. Berryhill, "West Tulsa, Okla.," *Pentecostal Evangel*, April 7, 1923, 10.
[53] "West Tulsa, Okla.," *Pentecostal Evangel*, March 14, 1925, 14.
[54] "West Tulsa, Okla.," *Pentecostal Evangel*, November 20, 1926, 22.

recalls that those early families were "willing to blaze a trail to bring the full gospel message to those who hadn't heard." [55] Later that spring, Pastor Hill of First Pentecostal Assembly of Redfork became ill, and the two groups merged to strengthen the Pentecostal witness in this area. In September 1936, Pastor H. T. Owens led the church to purchase a property at W. 48th Street and 31st. W. Avenue and named it Tulsa Gospel Center.

7.7 Carbondale Assembly of God, 1940s (Carbondale AG)

In 1940, Pastor F. C. Cornell changed the name to Carbondale Assembly of God.[56] The church moved to the present location at 2135 W. 51st in 1967 under Pastor H. D. Pieratt. He was followed by Pastor J. L. McQueen in 1975 who expanded the facilities. In 1985, Pastor Phil Taylor became pastor. His family joined the church in 1967 and Taylor was invited to be on staff with Pastor McQueen in 1976. Taylor is a talented musician and has published several books on the Holy Spirit. Under his leadership, the church has continued to be significant in the Tulsa area. The facility has undergone several remodels and expansions since Taylor became pastor, including the rebuilding of the church after a tornado significantly damaged the building in May of 1999.

---

[55] Phil Taylor, "Carbondale Connect," May 5, 2019, Carbondale Assembly of God, Tulsa, Oklahoma.

[56] My thanks to Pastor Phil Taylor, who has served as pastor since 1985, for providing these details as well as the anniversary brochure, "Carbondale Assembly of God: 75 Years," Carbondale Assembly of God, Tulsa, Oklahoma, 2008.

1st Pentecostal Church Garden City/Metro Pentecostal

The first Oneness Pentecostal church in Tulsa dates back to 1922. Today it is called Metro Pentecostal, but it was originally known as First Pentecostal Church of Garden City.[57] In 1922, a Oneness pastor named Arthur T. Duck came to the West Tulsa Assembly of God to hold a revival. When the pastor found out that Duck was preaching Oneness, he refused to allow him to preach. Instead, Duck began holding meetings in the Freewill Baptist Church in the area of Garden City near Elwood and 41st Street. As he preached the Oneness message, several accepted the teaching and were baptized in Jesus' name in the old coalmines (presently under the Tulsa Fairgrounds at 21st and Yale). One of the couples who accepted Duck's preaching was B. L. and Willie Lou Still. Willie Lou was the first to be baptized in Jesus' name. This caused a great stir in the Baptist church, and many left, but Brother Still also accepted the teaching and encouraged Duck to stay. The first church building was built in 1928. Thus began the First Pentecostal Church of Garden City.

7.8 **Arthur Duck and Apostolic Believers c. 1930s (Don Martin)**

In 1929, C. P. Williams, another important Oneness pastor, came to Tulsa and established the First Apostolic Church. Brother Still and Brother Duck joined with him. They built a brick building at 21st and Nogales that was completed in 1933. The church was a huge success and held many mighty revivals. In 1939, Williams established the Apostolic Bible School, a Oneness Bible School that trained many pastors around

---

[57] Adapted from "About Us/History," Metro Pentecostal Church, accessed December 18, 2020, https://metroupc.com/about-us/.

the nation.⁵⁸ In 1945, the United Pentecostal Church endorsed the Bible school. It eventually closed in 1960. First Apostolic eventually left the UPC and remained independent. Today, First Apostolic Church is at 6600 S. 33rd W. Avenue.

7.9 First Pentecostal Church, Garden City c. 1940 (Don Martin)

In 1941, B. L. Still left Williams to pastor the Garden City Church, which for a time had been pastored by Pastor Clarence Crain.⁵⁹ Still expanded the church on the property at 3623 S. Jackson Street. The church officially affiliated with the United Pentecostal Church in 1955. Still's son, Lloyd Still, followed him as pastor from 1960-1969. In 1973, Orville and Donna Bryant became pastor and relocated the church to Berryhill and renamed it Berryhill United Pentecostal Church.⁶⁰ In 2000, Pastor Don Martin became pastor and under his leadership the church took another step of growth. They moved the church to 8611 E. 21st Street in Tulsa at and renamed the church Metro Pentecostal Church. After several decades of blessing and growth, the church once again moved to South Tulsa where they purchased the Park Plaza Church of Christ building at 51st and Sheridan, which was officially dedicated on August 30, 2020.

---

⁵⁸ "Claiborne Price Williams," Apostolic Archives International Inc., accessed December 18, 2020, https://www.apostolicarchives.com/Rev_Clairborne_Price_Williams.html. See also "Our History," First Church, Tulsa Hills, accessed December 18, 2020, https://firstchurchtulsahills.com/whatwebelieve.

⁵⁹ Martin, *The First Pentecostal Church of Garden City*, 25-27.

⁶⁰ Garrison and Westberg, *Claiming the Land*, 236.

8

POST-WORLD WAR II CHURCHES

During the late 1930s, Tulsa was still recovering from the Great Depression. The struggling oil industry hurt the Tulsa economy, but the start of WWII gave a boost to the city. The 1940s proved pivotal to growing the cosmopolitan city. Suburbs expanded south of downtown, and the WPA helped build new schools to meet the educational needs of a growing suburbia. The airline industry provided well-paying jobs with McDonald Douglas making their home in Tulsa. The cultural community of Tulsa blossomed with museums and other forms of cultural entertainment. Tulsa was certainly coming of age as Tulsa became a great place to raise a family.

The prosperity of Tulsa also greatly helped Tulsa's Pentecostal community. By 1940, Tulsa had eleven Assemblies of God churches.[1] These churches enjoyed great unity during this era due to the efforts of H. T. Owens, pastor of Full Gospel Tabernacle, who organized an effort to build Sunday school programs. The result was that over 2,000 enrolled in Sunday school.[2] It was also in the 1940s that some of the other Pentecostal denominations that struggled to gain a footing in Tulsa started having success and planted new churches.

The 1930s–1940s were good years for the African American community. During the Great Depression, segregation insulated black businesses from some

---

[1] "Four Years of Phenomenal Growth in Tulsa," *Pentecostal Evangel*, April 15, 1939, 16. AG churches included North Peoria and Haskell (Capital Hill/Woodlake), Burner Station Assembly, Home Gardens Assembly, Tulsa Gospel Assembly, Full Gospel Tabernacle, Faith Mission Assembly, Glad Tidings Assembly, North Utica Assembly, Springdale Assembly, West Tulsa Assembly (Carbondale AG), and West Bowen Assembly.

[2] A. H. Argue, "The Value of Unity," *Pentecostal Evangel*, May 18, 1935, 6.

of the effects of the economic downturn, and Greenwood thrived. As Hannibal Johnson notes, "Segregation turned out to be a double-edged sword, at once a curse and a blessing, for the African American community."[3] In 1938, a group of African American men established the Greenwood Chamber of Commerce.[4]

The tragedy of 1921 and Jim Crow laws ensured that white and black Tulsa would be segregated for the next forty years. White Pentecostals did little to change that reality. Emblematic of this failure, a watershed moment in the racial divide in Pentecostalism took place during a convention held in Tulsa in 1937. For the first few decades of the twentieth-century, the Pentecostal Assemblies of the World was an integrated fellowship. That was until the 1930s, when most of the white ministers broke off to form white Oneness groups.[5] However, in 1931 a merger took place of several of the last Oneness groups that included black ministers, which formed the Pentecostal Assemblies of Jesus Christ.[6]

Because of the interracial nature of the PA of JC clergy, most of the meetings were held in northern states. However, in 1936, a resolution was passed that said it was unfair to southern ministers to always have to travel to the north. So in 1937, Tulsa Pastor, C. P. Williams, managed to persuade the leadership to hold the annual conference in Tulsa. This move, of course, alienated the black ministers in the group because Tulsa was a segregated city. This racially insensitive action by Williams and other leaders was the last straw for African American ministers. The following year, the remaining black members of the PA of JC left to rejoin the original Pentecostal Assemblies of the World. Emblematically, Tulsa was the site for the end of the last remaining racially integrated Pentecostal fellowship until the modern era.

Pentecostals continued to struggle with integration in Tulsa during the 1940s-1960s, when the African American community expanded beyond Greenwood into suburb areas of north Tulsa. These traditionally white neighborhoods, such as the 36th Street North corridor, were gaining more African American families. But,

---

[3] Johnson, *Black Wall Street*, 112.

[4] Johnson, *Black Wall Street*, 102.

[5] See Talmadge L. French, *Early Interracial Oneness Pentecostalism: G. T. Haywood and the Pentecostal Assemblies of the World* (Eugene, OR: Wipf & Stock, 2014).

[6] Arthur L. Clanton and Charles E. Clanton, *United We Stand* (Hazelwood, MO: Word Aflame Press, 1995), 96-97

instead of embracing their neighbors, whites fled south to avoid integration. Within the decade of 1950–1960, the 36th Street North area went from 91% white to 75% black.[7]

During the 1960s, civil rights advances opened new opportunities for blacks in Tulsa, both residential and commercial. African American wealth, no longer segregated, started flowing to white businesses. Within a decade Greenwood was no longer a viable business district. In the early 1960s–1970s, through the urban renewal initiative, the city bought black owned property and pushed black residents and businesses further north and east of downtown. When Interstate 244 was built through the heart of Greenwood, it created a physical barrier that ended Greenwood's commercial district. The interstate also served as social barrier that geographically divided the predominantly black North Tulsa and white South Tulsa. Despite the economic decline, churches continued to be the center of the community.

Greater Lansing Church of God in Christ

In the 1940s, Mother Ada Reily had a vision that Greater Lansing needed to have a new emphasis on growth. Over the next few years, the church rapidly progressed and services were packed under Elder A. L. Hearne's leadership. Elder Hearne also continued to be a steady source of leadership in the COGIC church in the Tulsa District, where he served as overseer for twenty-one years. Hearne retired from Greater Lansing COGIC after forty-eight years of service.[8] Mother Hearne also had a great impact on Oklahoma. She was instrumental in organizing the first state of Oklahoma Department of Women's Work. When Page wanted to create the state headquarters in Oklahoma City, Mother Hearne organized state fundraisers.

---

[7] White flight allowed black families to thrive, but the economic impact was devastating. See "36th Street North Corridor Small Area Plan," City of Tulsa Planning Division, 2013, accessed December 18, 2020, https://www.cityoftulsa.org/media/1560/36snc.pdf.

[8] "History of Greater Lansing Church of God in Christ," Greater Lansing Church of God in Christ," accessed December 18, 2020, https://www.greaterlansingcogic.org/history.

As the Oklahoma State Mother, she organized the first Missionary Institute and her long service to the Oklahoma work impacted many.[9]

In January 1978, Bishop Hearne appointed Elder Titus Robertson to serve as pastor. When the building at 1202 N. Lansing caught on fire, the church was faced with a decision. Hearne moved the church to its present location at 4909 N. Cincinnati. After Hearne passed away in 1983, Elder James W. and Daisy Ciggs, who also served New Bethel COGIC in West Tulsa, assumed the pastorate for two years. In July 1989, Superintendent Benjamin Borens, Sr. and his wife, Thermaple, took over in July 1989. They continued to expand the ministries of the church to minister to the needs of the community.

First Church of God in Christ

Began in 1917, First Church of God in Christ incorporated May 24, 1920.[10] Following the Massacre, they moved to 1249 N. Greenwood Avenue. The church continued to be the flagship church for Tulsa. During the 1950s, Elder A. T. Thompson served as the pastor and State Overseer for Northeast Jurisdiction. In 1957, under the leadership of Pastor J. A. Young, the church began working on a new brick building next door at 1251 N. Greenwood Avenue. This building has served the congregation for over a half-century. Other pastors have included Bishop Carl Prather, Bishop Hawkins, and Pastor E. J. Palmer. First Church started a Charles Mason Bible College, later called C. H. Mason Jurisdictional Institute, led by Missionary Frankie Lu Anderson.

---

[9] "Her Achievements," *Workshop '94: 44th State Women's Convention* (Tulsa, OK: Oklahoma Northwest Jurisdiction of the Church of God in Christ, 1994), 31. "Annual State Women's Convention, COGIC, Tulsa, Oklahoma, 1994," USC Libraries USC Digital Library: Pentecostal and Charismatic Research Archive (PCRA), accessed December 18, 2020, http://digitallibrary.usc.edu/cdm/compoundobject/collection/p15799coll14/id/239708/rec/16.

[10] "Entity Summary Information: Tulsa Church of God in Christ," Oklahoma Secretary of State, accessed December 8, 2020, https://www.sos.ok.gov/corp/corpInformation.aspx?id=1400033191.

8.1 First Church of God in Christ

Northside Church of God in Christ

During the Post WWII era, the north Tulsa residential community expanded. One important church that began during this era was Northside Church of God in Christ. Northside began in the early 1950s and one of the early pastors was Elder F. M. Campbell.[11] The church built a building at 1101 E. Apache that opened May 25, 1958 under Pastor C. Prather. Pastor Prather served as both pastor and Superintendent of Tulsa until the 1990s, and Mother Ruth Prather was head of the State Department of Women. Some of the other pastors who were district leaders have been Elder M. O. Ross and Supt. David A. Johnson. Dr. Johnson has led the church since the early 2000s and has been a steady source of leadership. In more recent years, Tulsa's COGIC churches continued to grow as the community grew. By the 1990s, Tulsa had nearly a dozen COGIC Churches: First Church, Northside, Greater Lansing, Gospel Tabernacle, Miracle Temple, Ark of Safety, Mason Temple, Bibleway, Victory Tabernacle, Emmanuel, and Solid Rock.

One famous group of musicians to come out of the Tulsa COGIC churches was the GAP Band, the 1970s R&B group. Founded in 1967, brothers Ronnie, Charlie, and Robert Wilson began singing together with their mother in various

---

[11] *The 47th-48th Annual Convocation, Church of God in Christ* (Memphis, TN: Church of God in Christ, 1954-1955), 63.

Pentecostal churches in Tulsa.[12] The brothers learned to play and sing in church from their gifted mother, Irma Wilson, the leader of the COGIC Music department in Oklahoma.[13] The three boys named their band "GAP Band," from the streets of their neighborhood—Greenwood, Archer, and Pine. While their Platinum selling funk and R&B albums departed from their Holiness upbringing, they are part of the rich heritage of musicians to come out of Tulsa.

Page Memorial Church of God in Christ

One of the most significant black Pentecostal churches in Tulsa during this era was Page Memorial Church of God in Christ. In 1943, J. L. (Jesse Lee) and Sister Alaman came to Tulsa and set up a tent on Greenwood where his dynamic preaching had a unique ability to draw crowds. In 1947, the church built a finished basement as the first phase of a permanent building at 448 E. Latimer Place. A few years later, with the help of other churches, Alaman was able to raise funds to finish the two-story building named Page Memorial after Bishop Page.

8.2 **Page Memorial Basement, c. 1950 (Jackie Alaman-Stoker)**

---

[12] Hugh W. Foley, Jr., "Gap Band," *Encyclopedia of Oklahoma History and Culture*, Oklahoma Historical Society, accessed November 21, 2020, https://www.okhistory.org/publications/enc/entry.php?entry=GA009.

[13] Charlie Wilson, *I am Charlie Wilson* (New York: Atria Books, 2015), 7.

Alaman was a significant figure in Tulsa's Pentecostal history. He was a popular speaker in both black and white circles. He held revivals during the 1950s across the nation and was one of the best-known black Pentecostal preachers in the nation. Alaman had the unique vision to bring together black and white pastors. In 1955, he hosted Tulsa's first interracial meeting. The meeting took place at 1022 N. Greenwood Avenue and was hosted by Page Memorial COGIC. The co-sponsors were white pastors F. G. Conley of Revival Tabernacle and A. D. Marney of Rays of Faith Tabernacle. With the help of these pastors, in 1959 Page Memorial built the two-story building that became a pillar in the community.[14]

8.3 Page Memorial Church of God in Christ, c. 1960 (Jackie Alaman-Stoker)

Alaman's dynamic leadership made Page Memorial one of the most popular Pentecostal churches in Tulsa. He continued to travel around the country holding services in white and black churches. He also had a local radio program. His high profile in Tulsa caught the attention of fellow revivalists, Oral Roberts and T. L. Osborn, both of whom befriended him. In turn, Alaman was a supporter of Oral Roberts University. He also started the Full Gospel Deliverance Association that credentials ministers across the nation and was associated with Apostle Arturo Skinner of Deliverance

---

[14] *Jackson Advocate*, February 12, 1955, 1; Newspaper Archive, accessed December 6, 2020, https://newspaperarchive.com/jackson-advocate-feb-12-1955-p-1/.

Evangelistic Center in Brooklyn, New York. Alaman passed away in 1969 while preaching a revival in Colorado.

8.4 J. L. Alaman, Preaching at Page Memorial (Jackie Alaman-Stoker)

Greater Grace & the Pentecostal Assemblies of the World

One of the earliest churches in the Pentecostal Assemblies of the World (PAW) was established in Skiatook, Oklahoma in 1915. However, it would take forty years until a PAW would be established in Tulsa. The PAW, a primarily Black, Oneness Pentecostal body, had its main concentration in the North Central United States. In 1955, Elder W. H. and Minnie Black started an Apostolic church at 1225 N. Kenosha and named it Pentecostals in Christ Jesus Church.[15] Elder Black had been serving in England, Arkansas when he felt God tell him to move to Tulsa. The church started only with three members, but over the next few decades, the church continued to grow. In 1975, they purchased a new building at 1019 E. 54th Street North and changed the name to Grace Apostolic Temple.

Elder Black was instrumental in founding the Oklahoma State Council of the PAW in 1958. Bishop Samuel J. Grimes appointed Bishop David T. Shultz to organize the territories of Arkansas, Texas, and Oklahoma. So in November 1958, Schultz organized a Bible Convention at the True Holiness Temple in Wewoka,

---

[15] "Oklahoma State Council 60 Years Diamond Jubilee 1958-2018," 26th Episcopal District of the Pentecostal Assemblies of the World, Oklahoma City, Oklahoma, 2018, 64.

Oklahoma, pastored by M. B. Cobb. In attendance was Elder Black, Elder Cobb, Elder E. I. Butcher of Lawton, B. L. Pitts of Oklahoma City, and Pastor Fannie Elmore of Stringtown. Together they formed the Oklahoma State Council. The first state convention was held in Tulsa in May 1959 at Elder Black's church.[16]

8.5 Pentecostal Church in Jesus Christ, Tulsa (PAW)

Elder Black served faithfully for several decades. In 1985, Grace Apostolic Temple had grown to over 200 members.[17] Many other pastors were mentored and served under Black until he passed away October 15, 1992. Mother Minnie Black assumed the pastoral duties until 1998. Mother Black received an honorary doctorate from Aenon Bible College in recognition of her tremendous leadership in the Oklahoma PAW. She passed away June 21, 2004.[18] In 1998, Dr. Donald O'Neil Tyler assumed the leadership of the church. Dr. Tyler's leadership has continued to grow the church and in 2011 built a 16,000-sf. faculty at 1010 E. 56th Street North.

The next PAW church to come into Tulsa was Refuge Temple of Praise, founded in the late 1970s by Pastor Isaiah Bucher. After several years of ministry, Bucher was succeeded by Bishop Luke Church, a native Tulsan and successful

---

[16] "Oklahoma State Council 60 Years Diamond Jubilee 1958-2018," 22-24.
[17] Ethel Trice, *The 70th Year Historical Souvenir Book of the Pentecostal Assemblies of the World* (Indianapolis, IN: Ethel Trice, 1985), 58, 177.
[18] "Oklahoma State Council 60 Years Diamond Jubilee 1958-2018," 64.

white PAW pastor in West Siloam Springs. In the 1990s, he returned to Tulsa to pastor Refuge Temple. When Church retired in 1998, Bishop Nelson and Veda McMillian became pastors and have been since 1998. Today they occupy a 350-seat facility at 1916 N. Archer.[19] The most recent PAW churches established in Tulsa are both pastored by women. Divine Inheritance Ministries at 3 N. Phoenix was founded in 2005 by Tulsa District Elder, Dr. Jessie M. Lazenby. New Birth Tabernacle at 4301 S. 45th W. Avenue, was founded in 2018 by Pastor Edna A. Johnson.[20]

Mother Grace Tucker Ministries

Mother Grace Tucker is a revered Tulsa icon with roots in COGIC who ministered to Tulsa's poor and homeless for over fifty years.[21] Mother Tucker was born in the all-black town of Tullahasee, Oklahoma in Wagoner County. During her tumultuous teen years, she was saved and baptized in the Holy Spirit at a holiness church in Okmulgee. Mother Tucker felt called into ministry and started holding her own youth revivals, but the COGIC does not allow women pastors. She eventually started her own church in the 1940s called Revival Center House of Prayer. In 1957, they built the church building, which stands today. Mother Tucker is recognized as the first black woman to pastor an integrated church in Oklahoma.[22]

In the early 1960's, Mother Tucker and her husband Otis moved back to Tulsa and started working among the poor. She founded Revival Center House of Prayer at 4501 W. 55th Place in the South Haven area of West Tulsa. She also became the first Black woman to have a radio program in the city. But she is best known for Mother Tucker Ministries, the benevolence ministry with food programs, homeless ministry, and women's home. In 2001, Oral Roberts

---

https://rtpnewdimension.wixsite.com/mysite/history

[20] https://www.oscfc.org/pastors.html

[21] Doyle Tucker, *The Mother Grace B. Tucker Story* (Tulsa, OK: Victory Publishing, 2012).

[22] Tim Stanley, "Pioneering Pastor 'Mother' Grace Tucker Dies at 93," *Tulsa World*, August 29, 2012. https://tulsaworld.com/news/local/pioneering-pastor-mother-grace-tucker-dies-at-93/article_b41ac5df-8f7f-5ead-9439-a70f0fbc5deb.html (accessed 26 February 2021).

University awarded Mother Tucker with an honorary doctorate for her service to the poor. The City of Tulsa also recognized her ministry and named a street after her in North Tulsa. Mother Tucker passed away in 2012 at the age of 93.

Church of the Silent Sheep

In 1948, the first deaf-mute Pentecostal congregation in Oklahoma was established as a home mission. The idea began in 1936 when Brother and Sister Meacham, deaf evangelists, began working among the deaf in Tulsa. When they left town for other fields, they turned the work over to LaVonna (Nell) Thompson. In 1944, God spoke to Thompson to build a church exclusively for the deaf. She began with only $17.00. Four years later, the church opened and was named "Church of the Silent Sheep" on January 11, 1948.[23] She later married Lloyd Vaughn. The church first began downtown at 4th and Cincinnati until Thompson moved the church to a building at Rockford and Admiral. She served for over fifty years in ministry to the deaf and for nine years ministered at the deaf camps in Sulphur, Oklahoma. In 1954, Pastor Gerry Tigert moved the church to meet in Central Assembly, and it was called Central Deaf Church. The church remained a part of Central Assembly until 1983. In 1986, Jimmy Schwyhart moved the church to Garnett Assembly and changed the name to Praise Assembly Deaf Church.[24]

Church of God

In May of 1930, the Church of God of Prophecy held a state convention in Tulsa, hosted by Pastor I. D. Bain, pastor of the West Tulsa Church of God at 2302 S. Quannah. Bain was the State Overseer for Oklahoma and responsible for many revivals in the Tulsa area including Coweta, Sapulpa, and Bristow. Prior to the Convention, Bain was having great success in West Tulsa, as he writes,

---

[23] "Deaf-Mute Church Dedicated," *Pentecostal Evangel*, February 28, 1948, 12-13.
[24] "Our History," Praise Assembly Deaf Church, accessed November 12, 2020, https://www.deafchurch.tv/our-history.html.

Some are getting through to victory almost every series and the power is falling in the old fashion way. We are now beginning to see that our building is too small but we expect to build on in the near future that will hold more people.[25]

Ministers from around Oklahoma came to hear General Overseer, A. J. Tomlinson, as well as guests from other states.[26] The meetings were met with enthusiasm and rejoicing as Brother Tomlinson shared about missions, "Bible order" and gave encouragement to continue the work of God in Oklahoma.[27] Mrs. R. D. Kelly recalls, "Almost all the afternoon was given over to the church and was spent in displaying banners, parades, singing and general rejoicing. It looked to me like the Church of God in Oklahoma actually stood on tip toes." As a result of the convention, forty-three new believers were added to Bain's West Tulsa church.

In 1944, Pastor A. B. Smith opened a Church of God (Cleveland, TN) in West Tulsa at 1610 S. Quanah, next to the Arkansas River.[28] They purchased a building vacated by a Free Holiness Church and began with only eight members.[29]

Pentecostal Holiness Church and Evangelistic Temple

Some of the very first Pentecostal churches in Oklahoma were Pentecostal Holiness Churches, and yet, there was not a single church in Tulsa until 1942, while there were eleven AG churches. This did not sit well with Bishop J. A. Synan who lamented that Oklahoma's second largest city was without a PH Church and felt burdened to get one started. So, in 1941, a conference for the Eastern Oklahoma Conference was scheduled with Oral Roberts slated as the speaker. However, when sickness caused Roberts to cancel, Oscar Moore was chosen to lead the meeting focusing on going door to door in an effort to start a Pentecostal Holiness Church

---

[25] I. D. Bain, "Oklahoma," *White Wing Messenger*, February 1, 1930, 2.
[26] "Specials, Coming Events," *White Wing Messenger*, May 10, 1930, 1-2.
[27] "Oklahoma Convention a Wonderful Feast," *White Wing Messenger*, July 5, 1930, 3.
[28] "Notices," *Church of God Evangel*, November 11, 1944, 2.
[29] "The Church of God Organized in Tulsa, Oklahoma," *The Church of God Evangel*, December 23, 1944, 14.

in the city.³⁰ Moore was already pastoring in Okmulgee and served as the Eastern Oklahoma Conference Superintendent. Through the efforts of Arthur Smith, pastor of the Sand Spring Church, they were able to finally establish a work in Tulsa. In December 1942, the *Pentecostal Holiness Advocate* paper declared, "Tulsa at Last!"³¹ G. H. Montgomery took to the Tulsa Radio airwaves to stir up interest, declaring, "I for one certainly believe this home Mission program will fit into this NEW PENTECOSTAL REVIVAL and we will see great results."³² Smith continued to pastor the Church until 1945 when he left to enter full-time evangelistic work.³³

Lee F. Hargis followed Smith in 1945 and made significant improvements to the church by raising $5,000 for renovations.³⁴ They added twenty-four feet to the length of the church, installed a baptistery, a choir loft, and new pews. They also added six Sunday school rooms. The church still struggled to draw a crowd for the Holiness-Pentecostal message, but Hargis was a notable preacher, and at times had success. Hargis served for a year until he left to engage in full-time evangelistic ministry.³⁵

In 1946, Steve Pringle of Memphis, Tennessee, became the pastor of the Pentecostal Holiness Church in Tulsa. Pringle was interested in the ministry of healing because both he and his son had dramatic healing experiences. When he arrived, he found a struggling church. He comments, "Our first Sunday in Tulsa was not so encouraging. There were less than forty people."³⁶ In an effort to grow the church, Pringle used all of his savings to buy a tent to hold a revival on an empty lot at 600 N. Main. His very first service in the tent, a lady was healed of cancer. This stirred the community and the crowds followed. Pringle then made a decision that would change the Pentecostal Holiness Church and Tulsa forever.

---

³⁰ "Special Notice," *Pentecostal Holiness Advocate*, April 3, 1941, 14. Cf. *Pentecostal Holiness Advocate*, April 24, 1941, 14.

³¹ "Tulsa At Last," *Pentecostal Holiness Advocate*, December 10, 1942, 7. emphasis original.

³² G. H. Montgomery, "The Minister as a Defense Worker," *Pentecostal Holiness Advocate*, December 10, 1942, 3, 14.

³³ G. H. Montgomery, "Entering Evangelistic Work," *Pentecostal Holiness Advocate*, May 24, 1945, 11.

³⁴ "Tulsa Church Enlarged, Improved," *Pentecostal Holiness Advocate*, February 28, 1946, 13.

³⁵ "Returns to the Field," *Pentecostal Holiness Advocate*, August 1, 1946, 15.

³⁶ Steve Pringle, "What Faith Means to Me," *Healing Waters*, October 1949, 6-7, 11.

In May of 1947, Oral Roberts moved to Tulsa to begin his healing ministry when Pringle invited him to preach a one-week revival in his tent at 600 N. Main. The first night, the one thousand-seat tent was only sparsely filled, but Roberts wasn't discouraged, recalling: "I was conscious of the anointing of the Holy Spirit. I was able to preach with the fire and the power of God upon me."[37] The next day, word spread of the healing power of God, and for the next three nights crowds of several hundred filled the tent to hear Roberts preach. His preaching drew both white and black Pentecostals, and he comments, "I was beginning to see what the ministry could do to bring people together. It blotted out the denominational barriers, color lines, and disunity."[38] But what happened next made national headlines. At one service, a man who complained about the noise of the Pentecostal meeting shot a gun into the tent, missing Roberts' head by eighteen inches. The story made headlines, and Oral Roberts became a national name.

Pringle's tent was located on an empty lot at the western base of Standpipe Hill, in between an upscale neighborhood to the west and the Greenwood District three blocks to the East. Next door was a large white building called Beno Hall where 3,000 members of Tulsa's KKK klavern had terrorized blacks in Greenwood until it closed in 1929. It was occupied by several other businesses including a Baptist church, but by 1940, the building was vacant.[39]

---

[37] Oral Roberts, *Expect a Miracle: My Life and My Healing Ministry* (Nashville: Thomas Nelson, 1995), 89.

[38] Roberts, *Expect a Miracle*, 90.

[39] Steve Gerkin, *The Hidden History of Tulsa* (Charleston, SC: History Press, 2014), 19-20.

8.6 Evangelistic Temple c. 1960s (HSRC)

Enthusiasm over Roberts' healing ministry succeeded in adding new members to the fledgling church. To accommodate all the new converts Pringle purchased the old Beno Hall and named the church Evangelistic Temple.[40] Steve Gerkin poetically notes that by occupying this former pillar of racism, the church symbolically reclaimed "the stained soul of Standpipe Hill." [41] Little did Oral Roberts know that this would be the beginning of a lifetime of ministry that would reclaim spaces of racial segregation within the Christian community.[42]

Evangelistic Temple continued to thrive through the 1950s and early 1960s. Roberts' immediate family also continued to worship in the Church. In 1967, Dan Beller came to pastor the congregation, and they began preparing to find a new home in South Tulsa. The church purchased property at 55th and Peoria in 1964. After experiencing tremendous growth under Beller, they built a new sanctuary in 1973. In 1982, they added an education wing and started a Christian school. Beginning with 200 believers, Beller grew the church to over 2,000 with multiple services. His leadership helped Evangelistic Temple become one of the strongest

---

[40] Dan Beller, "Evangelistic Temple Church, Tulsa, Oklahoma," a paper presented to Church Growth I, Fuller Theological Seminary, 1981, Evangelistic Temple file, Holy Spirit Research Center, Oral Roberts University, Tulsa, Oklahoma.

[41] Gerkin, *The Hidden History of Tulsa*, 119.

[42] Daniel D. Isgrigg, "Healing for all Races: Oral Roberts' Legacy of Racial Reconciliation in a Divided City," *Spiritus: ORU Journal of Theology* 4, no. 9 (2019): 227-56

Pentecostal Holiness Churches in the U.S.[43] In 2001, Beller was followed by Norm Wilkie, who in 2012 changed the name to SpiritLife Church. Today the church is led by Tommy McLaurin.

Beams of Light & Grace Gospel Churches

Grace Gospel Churches are a fellowship of Pentecostal churches with roots back to 1906 when A. S. Copley received the baptism in the Holy Spirit. In 1907, Copley moved to Kansas City and started the ministry of "Grace and Glory." In 1910, he served as associate editor of J. Roswell Flower's magazine, *The Pentecost,* until Flower turned the paper over to him in 1911 and he changed the name to *Graceand Glory*.[44] In 1912, Mary Bodie, a Pentecostal evangelist and Bible teacher, joined Copley in publishing the paper. This Pentecostal group was unique because it emphasized the concept of "Pentecostal grace." [45] They consider themselves to be non-denominational with a Pentecostal theology but have a Baptist view of grace. They emphasize the assurance of believer's salvation, whereas other Pentecostals did not.

In 1914, Andrew Turner came to the Tulsa area and ministered in Claremore, Bixby, Glenpool, and Keifer. Turner's work in Glenpool had the biggest impact, as the Grace Gospel church there dates back to Turner's revival. In the town of Yale, northwest of Tulsa, Mrs. John Combs started a Holiness church in 1915. Combs accepted Copley's teaching on grace and established a church in Yale, that became one of the strongest Grace Gospel churches in Oklahoma. Over the next two decades, Grace Gospel Assemblies were established in Yale, Bristow, and Glenpool. In 1920, C. E. Foster came to Tulsa to preach the Grace Gospel among Pentecostals there. A. J. Covington arrived in 1926. It was not until the 1940s,

---

[43] Shirley Spencer, "The IPHC Remembers Dr. Dan Beller," IPHC General Superintendent's Office, September 16, 2019, accessed December 18, 2020, https://iphc.org/gso/2019/09/16/the-iphc-remembers-dr-dan-beller/.

[44] I am deeply grateful to Diana Firey, who has archived much of the information on the Grace Gospel Churches. She shared with me many wonderful documents and history from this group. See her website http://www.fireytrails.com/FGGF_Archives.htm.

[45] This history is adapted from Orville Freestone, Jr., *Indelible Grace: An Account of Grace Pentecostal Assemblies* (Wheat Ridge, CO: Abundant Grace Fellowship, 1990).

however, that a lasting work was established in Tulsa. This was largely due to the ministry of Oliver W. Webb and his brother, Charles C. Webb.

In 1923, Charles and O. W. Webb were living in Western Oklahoma. O. W. Webb moved to Kansas City where he was filled with the Holy Spirit under A. S. Copley. He would become one of the most important leaders of the Grace Gospel churches in the US. In 1935, O. W. and Elsie Webb settled in Bristow, Oklahoma where he built the Bristow Gospel Tabernacle. In 1938, Webb started a children's home for abandoned children. He also started a daily radio broadcast in 1936 from Tulsa. When the war began, Webb struggled to afford the gas to travel from Bristow to Tulsa to record his program. One day when he was in town, he stopped by a mansion at 41st and Harvard. Webb felt compelled by the Lord to knock on the door. When the owner answered, he asked, "Is your house for sale?" The lady replied, "No." But Webb walked away knowing that this building would be perfect for moving his children's home. A month later, the owners reached out to him and asked, "Do you still want it?"

8.7 Beams of Light Children's Home (Diana Firey)

Immediately they bought it and moved his family to Tulsa. In 1946, Webb re-opened what became the largest privately owned children's home in the state.[46] They raised their children together with those in the children's home. Daughter, Ruth Webb Darr, a long-time friend of the author, remembers that it was like having "50 brothers and sisters." The number of children in the home led to the

---

[46] Freestone, *Indelible Grace*, 73.

city to build Eisenhower Elementary School. The home was considered as one of the best in the state. According to Orville Freestone, "His orphanage, with its home-like atmosphere, became a model for... children's homes in the state."[47] The Webbs were recognized leaders in Tulsa's Pentecostal community and friends of T. L. and Daisy Osborn who regularly spoke at Beams of Light Tabernacle. T. L.'s brother lived next door and was the caretaker for the grounds.

In 1944, O. W. Webb started Beams of Light Tabernacle at 1704 S. Harvard. This assembly became a leader among Grace Gospel churches for several decades. He also started a paper called *Beams of Light* and had an effective radio program. Webb's brother, Charles and his wife, Ema, moved to Sapulpa to start Beams of Light Mission about the same time. The Sapulpa church was located at 21 N. Elm in downtown, on the same block as the original 1917 Pentecostal mission located at 16 N. Elm Street. The building exists today as the Masonic Lodge. The Beams of Light church at 101 E. Murphy in Sapulpa continues to be the home of the Full Gospel Grace Fellowship.

8.8 Beams of Light Tabernacle (Diana Firey)

In 1951, Webb felt like it was time to find homes for all of the children and closed the Children's Home. In 1952, Webb hosted a convention at Beams of Light, and they incorporated the Full Gospel Grace Fellowship, something the Grace Gospel churches never did formally. In 1957, this group ordained more than one hundred ministers. One person who came from these ministers was Bob Yandian, who became the pastor of Grace Fellowship Church in 1980. Phil Johnson—who was serving as associate pastor at Sheridan Christian Center and

---

[47] Freestone, *Indelible Grace*, 64.

invited Yandian to join him at Grace Fellowship—founded the church in 1972.[48] O. W. Webb tragically died in an automobile accident in 1953 on the Turner Turnpike at the young age of forty-five.

The White Church in Broken Arrow

The oldest church in the Tulsa area is the White Church in Broken Arrow on 129th E. Avenue between 121st Street and 131st Street. Today the church is called Full Gospel Grace Assembly and is part of the Grace Gospel Fellowship. Its roots go back to 1875, when the small white church started by a Creek Indian, Daniel Childers. One of the early pastors was the famous Presbyterian pastor, Samuel Loughridge, who was also responsible for founding several other missions around Tulsa and Muskogee.[49] The church served the Creek people as both a church and a schoolhouse. The cemetery next door is one of the oldest in the area and many of the early Creek residents of Broken Arrow are buried there.

In 1928, the church was sold to C. O. Stafford, uncle of Dean Stafford, the present-day pastor of Full Gospel Assembly. At some point C. O. moved to California, and the church was boarded up. In the early 1950s, the Staffords returned to the homestead and re-opened the church. O. W. Webb assisted them with re-opening the church and even supplied a pastor. The church continued to be called the White Church, a mission of Beams of Light. In 1967, Dean Stafford became the pastor. The church changed the name during the Civil Rights era when Pastor Stafford received a phone call from someone asking if the church was "only for white folks."[50] Stafford renamed it Full Gospel Grace Assembly. Today the church continues to preach the full gospel grace message and the building has been established as a historical landmark.

---

[48] Bill Sherman, "Grace Church Pastor to Step down to Become Ministry Teacher," *Tulsa World*, May 26, 2012.

[49] Nancy [no last name listed on blog], "Reverend Loughridge," August 28, 2011, Tulsa Gal, accessed October 31, 2020, http://www.tulsagal.net/2011/08/reverend-loughridge.html.

[50] Bill Sherman, "Longevity Has a Purpose: Oldest Church Building was Named After Its White Paint," *Tulsa World*, June 23, 2007.

Bethel Temple/New Life Center

The story of Bethel Temple/New Life Center Assembly of God begins on May 1, 1942 when W. G. Burgess, P. W. Siebert and Naomi Wilkerson officially created a new Assembly of God church.[51] Originally meeting in the historic Tulsa Hotel, the members agreed to purchase a former ballet studio at 1202 S. Boulder for $14,000. The first full-time pastor was Clyde F. Ferguson, elected in May of 1944. From the original thirty members, the church quickly grew to over 200 under the leadership of C. F. Ferguson who stayed only one year. The church experienced a series of pastors who only stayed for short periods until in the summer of 1952, G. A. Uldin was elected pastor and served six fruitful years.

8.9 Bethel Temple

In March 1959, the church elected Taylor H. Davis of Dodge City, Kansas as pastor. Under his leadership an organ was purchased, air conditioning was installed, and new programs for kids and youth were started. The aging downtown church was hampered by limited parking and plans to relocate began. In June 1962, the congregation purchased an A-framed church at 41st and Harvard for $5,450. This property was built by Bethany Lutheran next to the former Beams of Light

---

[51] The Author served as pastor of this church from 2010 to 2017. One of the first things I did was write the history of the church. It was actually this process that first gave me the idea of writing this book a decade ago.

Children's Home. In July of 1965, Mrs. Webb sold that home to Bethel Temple, for use as a childcare center.

Earlier in 1954, Suburban Hills Assembly began with sixteen people meeting in a local school near 46th Street North and Peoria. The church purchased property at 3960 N. Hartford and a facility was built. In 1965, George E. Smith became the pastor and the church grew. In the late 1960s, uncomfortable with the increase of the black population, Smith and the white congregation abandoned the Suburban Hills to move south.

In 1970, Smith joined Davis at 41st and Harvard in a unique church merger where they served as co-pastors. This arrangement worked well for a year and a half until in July of 1972, Davis and Smith both resigned. On August 6, 1972 and the congregation called Vernon L. McNally as their next pastor. The young McNally had a vision for a new kind of AG church and the church quickly grew from 200 to 300 in a matter of months.

The key to the church's success was its ability to reach younger families and ORU students. It also opened a counseling center, using skilled professionals and a Christian day care center. In January 1974, McNally started construction on the "New Life Center" at a cost of nearly $800,000, a large investment for the church its size. When it opened, New Life Center became the official name for the congregation. Due to the church's financial difficulties, McNally served only a few years after the building was built.

In December of 1977, the district leadership appointed James B. Holder—Youth Pastor at Broken Arrow Assembly under James Dodd—to the position of pastor. Holder brought new life and energy characterized by contemporary music, community outreach, and family-centered ministry, to the struggling church. Under his ministry, the church which had dwindled to congregation sixty steadily grew from a to an average of 250–300. The Christian day care center grew to over 120 children.

8.10 Bethel Temple/New Life Center

In 2000, Holder and the church leadership made a decision to again relocate to 5100 S. Aspen in Broken Arrow. The first services were held in the new 10,800-square-foot building in 2002. The new location brought new energy and financial freedom to the church. The church rebuilt with new families from the community and made great efforts to serve their new neighbors. In 2009, James Holder retired after thirty-two years as pastor.

In 2010, my wife Amonda and I were chosen to lead New Life Center. Over the next seven years, we focused on being a Spirit-filled church that was multi-generational and community focused. In 2016 the church changed its name to Aspen Creek Assembly. After seven years, in 2017, I stepped down to finish my Ph.D. degree and Bob Roach was elected to serve as the new pastor.

Sheridan Christian Center

Few mid-century churches have had more impact on Charismatic ministry in Tulsa than Sheridan Christian Center. Begun in 1951, Sheridan Road Assembly of God was founded by well-known AG leader, Glenn Millard.[52] The church began in a one-room garage, but quickly grew to 270 people. As they built a new building at 201 S. Sheridan, the church eventually reached 700 Pentecostal believers. It had a broad appeal to both Pentecostal and the newer Charismatic churchgoers in the

---

[52] McCloud and Thompson, *Journey*, 46.

1960s. In 1965 Vep Ellis, Jr., son of Vep Ellis, Sr., the music director for Oral Roberts Crusades, joined the staff as music director. He later served as music director at Rhema Bible Training Center in 1978.⁵³

Sheridan Christian Center c. 1960 (Sheridan Church)

Sheridan Assembly had a vision to raise up ministers to plant new churches around Tulsa. In 1967, Millard sent seven families to help J. W. Ellsworth start Eastland Assembly of God in East Tulsa.⁵⁴ Grace Fellowship was also started in 1972 by Millard's son-in-law, Phil Johnson, Bob Yandian, and a core group of families. The church was the home of Kenneth Hagin's first campmeetings in the late 1970s, and his Rhema Bible Training Center.

In the 1970s, Sheridan Assembly took a tremendous step forward in influence and notoriety when Billy Joe Daugherty became pastor in 1976. Daugherty had attended Oral Roberts University and served as a youth pastor at Sheridan before becoming its pastor in 1976. Under Daugherty, the church hosted two Bible schools, started a radio program, and opened a Christian school. By 1980, the

---

⁵³ Bill Sherman, "Vep Ellis, Longtime Sheridan Christian Center Pastor, Retires," *Tulsa World*, January 28, 2017, accessed October 31, 2020, https://tulsaworld.com/news/local/vep-ellis-longtime-sheridan-christian-center-pastor-retires/article_fe627ec6-1ad1-55e1-9ebc-03670c5d5730.html.

⁵⁴ Cathy Spaulding, "Church Marks 40 Years," *Tulsa World*, November 16, 1991, accessed November 20, 2020, https://tulsaworld.com/archive/church-marks-40-years-sheridan-christian-grows/article_26e03719-ade3-5200-9936-c38c14a2e6df.html.

church had outgrown the facility. When Daugherty wanted to move the church, the elders decided that, instead, he should start a second congregation, Sheridan Victory Christian Center.[55]

Daugherty's departure hurt the church, but Vep Ellis, Jr. returned to the renamed Sheridan Christian Center as pastor in 1984, and the church quickly regained its strength. The church carried on as an independent church for a number of years but rejoined the Assemblies of God. The church today is called Sheridan Church led by Jackson Lahmeyer located at 41st and Sheridan.

In early 1981, Daugherty purchased the Tink Wilkerson auto dealership at 4400 S. Sheridan for $3.3 million and on April 19, of that year, the congregation opened Victory Christian Center with 1600 people. They also opened Sheridan Christian School with 750 students and Victory Bible Institute with 1,200 students. Within a year, the church doubled in size, and decided that a new sanctuary was needed. In 1984 it moved to a vacant junior high school and in 1988 bought land across from ORU, while they held services in the ORU Mabee Center.

Church of God of the Apostolic Faith

Though the Church of God of Apostolic Faith had early roots around Tulsa, it took several years before the city had a permanent COGAF presence. In 1933, new works were started in Sapulpa and in Tulsa near Sand Springs.[56] In 1937, after his family home and everything they owned burned down. O. H. Bond moved to Bixby and published the *Apostolic Faith Messenger* paper from there.[57] Though many of Bond's extended family lived in Tulsa, the primary churches continued to be in Ramona (Happy Hill) and Sapulpa. There was also a church in Broken Arrow at the White Church. In 1940, a permanent camp was secured near Stillwell for a summer ministry to youth and children.[58]

---

[55] Spaulding, "Church Marks 40 Years."

[56] *Apostolic Faith Messenger,* June 1933, 6.

[57] O. H. Bond, "Our Recent Disaster!" *Apostolic Faith Messenger,* November 1937, 5.

[58] Ernest Buckles, "A Brief History of the Church of God, of Apostolic Faith," Anderson, MO, 1964, Church of God of the Apostolic Faith Collection, Holy Spirit Research Center, Oral Roberts University, Tulsa, OK.

Finally, in March 1943, a number of COGAF saints, including Will Aaron and Wilson Henegar, opened a mission at 822 W. 1st Street.[59] The start of the mission was hampered because the old building that needed upgrades and repairs.[60] By November, Wilson Henegar purchased a building at 4121 W. 5th Street [61] that offered spacious rooms and easy access on the Sand Springs streetcar line. That same month, Henegar began his evangelistic ministry, passing the church to L. L. Wheeler, who held a dedication service for the church in May of 1946. Other pastors who served the congregation include Cleo Atchley, Georgie Minick, and Brother Phillips.

Following the death of E. A. Buckles in 1935, the General Chairman position was passed to P. A. "Arlis" Henegar of Hobbs, New Mexico.[62] Henegar was a well-known evangelist who was ordained in Drumright in 1924. He had pastored in Ramona at Happy Hill as well as at other COGAF churches.[63] He served until 1952, and was succeeded by J. L. Sullivant, who was elected February 3, 1953 and served as Chairman until 1979.[64] Sullivant's father was one of the charter members of COGAF, and his mother was an ordained minister. [65] In 1955, Sullivant established an official COGAF office in the garage of his downtown Tulsa residence at 2526 W. Cameron just off Gilcrease Road near Sand Springs. The formal records he kept for the churches and ministers were donated to Oral Roberts University in 1968 and are preserved in the Holy Spirit Research Center. In 1979, the COGAF headquarters moved to 13334 E. 14th Street and today operates out of the Happy Hill Church in Romona, Oklahoma, where Jack Richey is pastor.

There are several unique aspects of the COGAF history. First, women played a significant role as pastors. In the 1930s-1950s, Isibell King and Ruby Steele co-pastored multiple churches including Happy Hill, Webb City, and Inola Oklahoma

---

[59] "New Work in Tulsa, Okla.," *Apostolic Faith Messenger*, March 1943, Supplement, 2.

[60] "Mother's Day in Tulsa," *Apostolic Faith Messenger*, May 1943, 8-9

[61] "New Church Location at Tulsa," *Apostolic Faith Messenger*, November 1943, 7.

[62] "Life Story," *Church of God Herald*, December 1945, 3.

[63] "Life Story of our Leader," *Church of God Herald*, November 1945, 2, 4.

[64] *Conference Minutes of the Church of God of Apostolic Faith*, Webb City, OK, February 3-5, 1953, 1. Holy Spirit Research Center, Oral Roberts University, Tulsa, OK.

[65] *Church of God of Apostolic Faith Newsletter*, October 1977, Church of God of the Apostolic Faith Collection, Holy Spirit Research Center, Oral Roberts University, Tulsa, OK.

and a church in Joplin, Missouri. Vida Austin served as pastor of Hickory Grove Church near Grove, Oklahoma. This phenomenon of female co-pastors was common, as unmarried women were ordained, but once they married, they were "taught not to usurp authority over the man."[66] A second unique aspect has been their consistent stance on armed conflict. Like most early Pentecostals, the COGAF adopted strict prohibitions against war and armed conflict. Unlike other Pentecostal groups who changed these views following WWII, however, COGAF has maintained a peace witness throughout its existence.

Christian Chapel Assembly of God

A final church was started much later in history, but is relevant to the Pentecostal community in Tulsa. My wife Amonda and I served on staff of Christian Chapel, founded in 1974 by Jonathan Wakefield, a student in the pioneer class at Oral Roberts University, and his wife, Janice. After graduation, the couple worked in Europe with Teen Challenge. After returning to Tulsa in 1974, they joined Alan and Doris Repko to start a new contemporary Assemblies of God congregation. Capturing the Charismatic ethos they had experienced at ORU, they envisioned a church that embraced contemporary worship and focused on supporting missions around the world.

The church was an immediate hit with ORU students and young couples. Within a couple of years, it grew from six people in the Wakefields' living room to over 300 in attendance in a storefront at 62nd and Lewis. With the growing congregation, they also for a short time met in Mason High (today Metro Christian School). In 1977, they purchased property at 91st and Memorial. Raising funds for a new facility proved difficult in the economic times of the late 1970s and they struggled to complete the project. Wakefield eventually stepped down in 1980 and he later started Harvest Church (AG) in Tulsa, the church he continues to pastor today.

In October 1980, Richard Exley assumed leadership of a congregation in flux. Through his leadership the church re-gained its financial strength by selling the

---

[66] Buckles, "A Brief History of the Church of God, of Apostolic Faith," 2.

property. Recommitted to support missions, Exley opened a Missionary in Residence home for furloughed missionary families. Then, through a gift of $429,000, the congregation purchased property on 76th Street between Sheridan and Memorial, built a 25,000-square-foot facility, and held its first service on Easter 1985.

Exley soon became an ecumenical leader, one of the most recognizable pastors in Tulsa. He hosted a popular radio broadcast, "Straight from the Heart," published several books, and had numerous opportunities to travel and speak for missions and renewal services. The congregation was on the forefront of the Tulsa pro-life movement, which helped birth the Crisis Pregnancy Outreach ministry in 1984. In the late 1980s, Christian Chapel became known for its seminars on Holy Spirit gifts, prophecy, and spiritual renewal, which brought tremendous growth. Exley left Christian Chapel in December 1992 to pursue his writing and speaking ministries. He was followed by Greg Cox, who served from 1993–1995.

8.11 Christian Chapel Assembly of God c. 1985 (Christian Chapel)

In 1995, Christian Chapel chose Greg Davis to be the new pastor. Greg and Donna Davis had attended Christian Chapel since 1977 and played an active role in church leadership serving as Worship Pastor, Associate Pastor, and Interim Pastor. His tenure was marked by a strong investment in children and youth. He also led two building programs—a Youth Center in 1997 and the addition of CPO Offices, classrooms, and a gym in 2010. The congregation built a new Missionary in Residence House in 1995 across from the church facility. During these years CC expanded its strong support of missions and helped start the first Royal Family

Kids Camp ministry in Oklahoma in 1999. I served under Davis as the Children's Pastor and Associate Pastor for twelve years.

Chris Dow became Christian Chapel's Lead Pastor in 2013. Having served as youth pastors since 2005, Chris and Angie Dow had already deeply invested in the congregation. But under their leadership, the church has grown numerically and expanded its ministries and community impact. Dow has a strong teaching gift and a heart for those who are lost and disconnected from God.

9

TULSA'S HEALING MINISTRIES

During the 1950s, Tulsa's Pentecostal community was thriving and the city became headquarters for some of the biggest names in the Healing Movement. Evangelists like Oral Roberts and Kenneth Hagin helped put Tulsa on the map as a vibrant location for Christian ministries. During the 1960s-1970s, independent ministers were breaking from Pentecostal denominations to form independent ministries, creating the beginning of the independent Charismatic Movement. These Charismatic churches influenced a whole new generation of Spirit-filled believers through a brand of Pentecostal spirituality that was not bound by denominational restrictions. While this period deserves its own dedicated volume, it's important to highlight the major figures who shaped Tulsa's Pentecostal landscape.[1]

Jack Coe

Few people know that the famous mid-century healing evangelist, Jack Coe, has roots in the Tulsa area. Coe was born March 11, 1918 in Oklahoma City, but during his early years his family moved to New York. His father was an industrious man who struggled with gambling, eventually lost everything and left the family. His mother went to Pennsylvania and worked small jobs, just barely getting by. A few years later, his father returned after he made some money in the oil fields of Oklahoma. The couple reconciled and they made their home in Sapulpa. But his

---

[1] The inclusion of these Charismatic ministries is focused on those that directly emerged from Pentecostal circles. The broader story of the 1960s-1970s Charismatic Renewal in mainline Protestant and Catholic churches is an equally important story that deserves its own study.

father soon returned to his gambling ways and was often away from the family for days or weeks. With five children and a myriad of her own difficulties, Coe's mother placed her children in the Creek County Children's Home in Sapulpa in 1927 when Coe was nine years old.[2] He remembers, "I thought my heart would break within me as I saw her going down that walk. For a long time I stood and cried." She came often to see him, but she never took him back and eventually moved to California.[3]

In 1935, at age of seventeen, Coe left the orphanage, living in various places around Sapulpa and Tulsa. He became a heavy drinker and was into all kinds of vices. After his doctor warned him that he was drinking himself to death, Coe decided to turnover a new leaf. He went to California to find his mother, but quickly fell into his old vices. After collapsing and being hospitalized, to make a fresh start, he moved to Fort Worth, Texas, accompanied by his mother who was determined to keep him sober. There he got a job managing a Singer Sewing company, but his life was still out of control until he visited a Nazarene church where he was saved. A year later, Jack moved back to Sapulpa where he managed the Singer Sewing agency in Tulsa between 1938-1940 and attended a Nazarene church.[4] His sister invited him to attend a Pentecostal campmeeting with her. Leading the meeting was a man named Jimmy Rogers. Coe describes the scene that took place in that old wood framed barn-like building:

> The church itself looked like an old barn. … The floor was covered in sawdust. … They had an orchestra. It consisted of a clarinet that a man hummed through. I sat down in a seat and thought, "this poor bunch" … A woman behind me kept saying "send the fire; Lord send the fire." Some fellow in front said, "Lord send the rain; Lord send the rain." Finally I turned around and asked, "Sister, what do you want, fire or rain?" She jumped up

---

[2] *Oklahoma Report of the Commissioner of Charities and Corrections* (Oklahoma City: State of Oklahoma, 1925), 114, mentions that the home had seventeen children and was run by Mrs. Bessie Beasley. Mrs. C. E. Edgerton was chair of the board. The report notes, "This is a most excellent Children's Home with Mrs. Bessie Beasley in church as Matron. She is a real mother to these children and they love her dearly" (97).

[3] Jack Coe, *The Story of Jack Coe: From Pup Tent to World's Largest Gospel Tent* (Dallas, TX: Herald of Healing, 1955) 18-24.

[4] Juanita Coe, *The Jack Coe I Know* (Dallas, TX: Herald of Healing, 1956), 14.

and said, "Both of them!". . . People would shout, and sometimes someone spoke in a language I didn't understand.[5]

Puzzled by what he saw, especially the speaking in tongues and shouting, Coe went the next day to talk to his Nazarene pastor who told him to stay far away from the "Holy Rollers" and that he only needed to speak in tongues if he was a missionary. The next day, when his sister asked if he was going again. He replied, "That thing is of the devil." However, later that night he couldn't sleep and decided to get up and go. Coe found his way to the altar and the saints prayed with him to let go of everything so God could fill him. The next night he returned to the altar, and at 4:00 a.m. Jack Coe received the baptism in the Holy Spirit.[6]

Over the next few years, Coe enrolled in Southwestern Assemblies of God Bible School led by P. C. Nelson in Waxahachie, Texas. Nelson took an interest in Coe and believed he would be a great minister. However, the United States was drawn into WWII and Coe joined the U.S. Army. When he returned in 1944, he resumed his ministry as an evangelist in the Assemblies of God.

A confident, almost brash, preacher, Coe appealed to plain folk audiences. The miracles performed in his meetings were second to none, as he seemed to effortlessly pray for the sick. Coe was quickly embraced by the Voice of Healing family and became a one of the movement's most famous healing evangelists. Historian David Harrell notes, "[o]f all the charismatic evangelists, only Jack Coe seriously challenged Oral Roberts as the popular leader of the revival."[7] Being from the Tulsa area, it was no surprise that Jack Coe came to Tulsa during an Oral Roberts 1951 revival to measure his tent so he could build one larger than Roberts.[8] Coe established his headquarters in Dallas, Texas while he continued to lead massive crusades around the nation in his "World's Largest Tent." His experience as an orphan so deeply impacted him that he opened the Herald of Healing Children's Home for orphans. When Coe suddenly passed away in 1956 at the age

---

[5] Coe, *The Story of Jack Coe*, 20.

[6] ibid., 26.

[7] David E. Harrell, Jr., *All Things Are Possible: The Healing & Charismatic Revivals in Modern America* (Bloomington, IN: Indiana University Press, 1975), 58.

[8] ibid., 59.

of thirty-eight, his wife, Juanita, continued his ministry and his publication, *Herald of Healing*.

Mildred Wicks

9.1 Mildred Wicks (HSRC)

For a short time, Tulsa was home to one of the most important female evangelists of the mid-century Healing Revival. Mildred Wicks was ordained in the Pentecostal Holiness Church and was a dynamic preacher who pastored churches across Oklahoma, including Cromwell, Kiowa, and Westville. Born in New Mexico, at age eighteen she was filled with the Holy Spirit at an Assemblies of God campmeeting on August 9, 1931.[9] On December 9 of that year, Wicks preached her first revival, and nearly 200 people came to Christ.

She married Albert Samuel Wicks on January 14, 1932. Sam was born in Braggs, Oklahoma and was a newspaper publisher. In 1938, Mildred Wicks was chosen as pastor of the Pentecostal Holiness Church in Westville, a small town on the Eastern border of Oklahoma on the route from Siloam Springs to Muskogee. She followed Oral's father, Ellis Roberts who had pastored for a year before her. Westville was also the home church of Evelyn Roberts.

Wicks and Oral Roberts were good friends who grew up together as young ministers in the Oklahoma Pentecostal Holiness circles. When Roberts took his first pastorate in Fuquay Springs, North Carolina, he invited Wicks to come for a revival in March 1942.[10] As one of her biggest fans, Roberts commented,

> I have never heard any better or more inspired preaching than was delivered by Sister Wicks. Her deeply spiritual ministry, her intensely prayerful life, her queenly walk and anointed sermons served to break down prejudice,

---

[9] "Rev. Mildred Francis Horn Wicks," Find a Grave, accessed October 21, 2020, https://www.findagrave.com/memorial/5647419/mildred-francis-wicks.

[10] "Revival at Fuquay Springs, N.C.," *Pentecostal Holiness Advocate*, February 12, 1942, 15.

indifference, lukewarmness and persecution and led the way for a soul ingathering revival.[11]

Over the next few years, both Roberts and Wicks were regular speakers at revivals and campmeetings in the Eastern and Western districts of the Pentecostal Holiness Church. Dan Beller, who became the pastor of the Pentecostal Holiness Church in Tulsa in 1967 was one person saved in a Wicks revival in Ada.

Throughout the early years, Wicks and Roberts often followed each other as pastor at several various churches. When Roberts left Fuquay Springs in 1943, Wicks was named pastor. In September of that year Wicks became the pastor of the Pentecostal Holiness Church in Newnan, Georgia.[12] When she left, Roberts followed her, as pastor for a few weeks until she returned as pastor. In 1947, Roberts and Wicks teamed up for one of Roberts' first healing crusades at their old church in Newnan, Georgia. The report called it "the greatest revival in the history of the Newnan church."[13] Together, they ministered to the crowd of over 700 people nightly, laying hands on the sick in a healing line that stretched around the building for hours. This service demonstrated that both would to be leaders in the healing ministry. Shortly after, both Roberts and Wicks made their ministry home in Tulsa.

Roberts often promoted Wicks in his magazine, *Healing Waters*. In 1950, Roberts said again of Wicks, "Sister Wicks is perhaps the greatest woman preacher on the field today. She is a great soul-winner and mighty miracles of healing are wrought through her ministry."[14] By 1953, Wicks had joined the Gordon Lindsey's Voice of Healing ministries as one of only two women actively promoted in the *Voice of Healing Magazine*. While she served in Tulsa for only a short time, she had a significant impact in Oklahoma. In many ways, without Mildred Wicks, there would be no Oral Roberts.

---

[11] Oral Roberts, "Great Revival at Fuquay Springs," *Pentecostal Holiness Advocate*, April 16, 1942, 13-14.

[12] "Mildred Wicks Georgia Pastor," *Eastern Oklahoma Conference News*, September 1943, 5.

[13] "Healing Revival in the Newnan Church," *Pentecostal Holiness Advocate*, July 17, 1947, 10.

[14] "Last Days Revivals," *Healing Waters*, October 1950, 14.

Oral Roberts

Oral Roberts was born in 1918 in Bebee, Oklahoma, a small town outside of Ada where his parents, Ellis and Claudius Roberts, were saved in Dan and Dolly York's Pentecostal meetings. Convinced of Pentecost, Ellis sold his 160-acre farm to enter full-time ministry and joined the Pentecostal Holiness Church to establish churches in Oil Center, Bebee, and Ada.[15] Oral was healed of tuberculosis in 1935 at a tent meeting near Ada held by Church of God evangelist, George Moncey. Shortly after his healing and Spirit baptism, the younger Roberts joined his father in evangelistic meetings around Oklahoma. When Oral received his license as a Pentecostal Holiness minister at the age of eighteen, he was ready to launch out on his own.[16] Oral met Evelyn at the annual IPHC campmeeting in 1936. She was from Westville, Oklahoma where her stepfather, Ira Fahnstock, was a minister. After finishing high school Evelyn was studying to be a school teacher when she took a job teaching in Texas where Oral visited her there and asked her to marry him. They were married December 25, 1938 in Westville where Mildred Wicks was the pastor.

9.1 Oral, Evelyn, and Rebecca Roberts c. 1940 (HSRC)

---

[15] E. M. and Claudius Roberts, *Our Ministry and Our Son Oral* (Tulsa, OK: Oral Roberts, 1960), 14-15.

[16] Daniel D. Isgrigg, "'I Tried Poverty': Exploring the Psychological Impact of Poverty and Prosperity in the Life of Oral Roberts," *Spiritus: ORU Journal of Theology* (2020): 16-17.

During his first three years as an evangelist, Roberts reported over 400 saved, 125 sanctified, and ninety-eight received the baptism in the Holy Ghost.[17] Despite his success and growing popularity, the couple and young daughter managed only a subsistence living.[18] To provide more for his family, Roberts accepted his first pastorate at an independent Pentecostal church in Fuquay Springs, North Carolina, in November of 1941. In the spring of 1942, Roberts and Wicks held a three-week revival in which fifty-three were saved, eighteen were sanctified, and three "went through" to the baptism in the Holy Ghost.[19] Roberts' stay in Fuquay Springs was short, and in September 1942 he accepted an assignment to pastor the Pentecostal Holiness Church in Shawnee, Oklahoma.[20] According to historian, Vinson Synan, Roberts was already showing that he was on his way to "a bright future in the denomination."[21] He enrolled in Oklahoma Baptist University and in 1945 even contemplated becoming a missionary to Palestine.[22]

In 1946, Roberts became the pastor of the Enid Pentecostal Holiness Church, but his time there was short-lived as Roberts was deeply unhappy with his ministry. He enrolled in Phillips University in Enid, hoping to finish his education. During a sociology class, he heard God speak: "Son, don't be like other men. Don't be like any denomination. Be like Jesus and heal like he did."[23] From that moment, Roberts determined that he would take God's message of healing to his generation. He held his first crusade in Enid that May—to great success. Lines of people

---

[17] *The East Oklahoma Conference News*, October 5, 1939, 1. Cf. Daniel D. Isgrigg and Vinson Synan, "An Early Account of Oral Roberts' Healing Testimony," *Spiritus: ORU Journal of Theology* 3, no. 2 (2018): 168-77.

[18] Roberts, *Expect a Miracle*, 53.

[19] Oral Roberts, "Great Revival at Fuquay Springs," *Pentecostal Holiness Advocate*, October 22, 1942, 15.

[20] Roberts, *Expect a Miracle*, 54; Taking the Shawnee Church was a sacrifice at first, but by the time Roberts had been there a year he had already seen several wage increases and even noted in the *EOCN* that his salary was the highest in the area at $40 per week. *The East Oklahoma Conference News* 6, no. 2 (October 1943), 4.

[21] Vinson Synan, "Oral Roberts: Son of Pentecostalism, Father of the Charismatic Movement," *Spiritus: ORU Journal of Theology* 2, nos. 1-2 (2017): 8.

[22] Daniel D. Isgrigg, "Oral Roberts: The (Almost) Missionary to Palestine," April 17, 2020, https://danieldisgrigg.com/2020/04/17/oral-roberts-the-almost-missionary-to-palestine/ (accessed 12 March 2021)

[23] Roberts, *Expect a Miracle*, 75.

waited for prayer for healing. His success confirmed that he was to resign his church and go back to full-time evangelistic healing ministry.

Having decided to leave the Enid church, Oral and Evelyn had to decide where they would live. His parents, Ellis and Claudius were living in Sand Springs, where they were pastoring a Pentecostal Holiness Church. His friend, Oscar Moore, who was living in Tulsa trying to start a new Pentecostal Holiness Church, invited the Roberts to visit. Since Roberts was leaving Enid, Moore took Roberts' place and offered to let the Roberts live in their home.[24] Oral purchased the home, which became the beginning of Healing Water ministries in 1947.

The first crusade Roberts held with Steve Pringle at 600 N. Main was the beginning of his significant impact on Tulsa. His ministry began out of his house at 1147 N. Main. But when he could no longer keep up with the mail, he opened a small building in Tulsa with the sign "Healing Waters Magazine." As Roberts' popularity grew, he built a massive headquarters building at 1720 S. Boulder to house his publishing ministry and his large ministry staff. The colossal square, windowless building was built in 1958 and designed by Tulsa architect, Cecil Stanfield. It was donned with diamonds, which symbolized "broken arrows, the symbol of peace."

9.3 Abundant Life Building (HSRC)

With Roberts' popularity came a greater need for space and privacy. He purchased a 280-acre farm on 121st and Mingo in Bixby and named it "Robin

---

[24] Roberts, *Expect a Miracle*, 87-89.

Hood Farms." From 1952-1958, the four Roberts children—Rebecca, Ronald, Richard and Roberta—were raised by Evelyn as Oral was gone for weeks at a time.

One day, while driving home from the downtown OREA office, Oral eyed a plot at 81st and Lewis and dreamed he would be able to buy the property for a ministry training school. In 1958, the Roberts moved back to Tulsa into the John D. Mayo home, a five-acre home at 2513 E. 38th Street.[25] This would be their home until the decision was made to build Oral Roberts University.

9.4 Roberts Family c. 1955 (HSRC)

Oral loved Tulsa, and Tulsa loved Oral and the ministry became a pillar of the community. As he spoke in 1956,

> I am a Tulsan. I love Tulsa, and I am one of the chief boosters of this city has around the earth. ... I believe that Tulsa is the most progressive, alert, modern minded city on the face of the earth.[26]

In the 1950s-1960s, Roberts was invited to be part of the Chamber of Commerce, Rotary Club, and The Down Town Civitan Club. In 1972, Roberts was elected to the Oklahoma Hall of Fame and during the 1960s and 1970s, he became one of Tulsa's favorite sons. Celebrities loved him and wanted to be his friends, and local

---

[25] David E. Harrell, *Oral Roberts: An American Life* (Bloomington, IN: Indiana University Press, 1985), 193-94.

[26] "Oral Roberts Chamber of Commerce Speech," March 1, 1956, ORU Archives, accessed December 18, 2020, https://digitalshowcase.oru.edu/or_speeches/7/.

and national politicians curried his favor. David Harrell notes that Oral Roberts Ministries, and ultimately ORU, was "one of Tulsa's most valuable economic assets, pumping $8 million annually into the city's economy."[27]

Oral Roberts University

One cannot think of Tulsa without thinking about the iconic campus of Oral Roberts University. Its architecture is as famous as its founder. At one time in the 1970s, ORU was one of the top destinations for tourists in Oklahoma. In fact, millions of Americans were introduced to Tulsa because of Oral Roberts' high profile. As significant as Oral Roberts' ministry was to the city, it is Oral Roberts University that has made a lasting impact on the global Spirit-empowered movement.

The Holy Spirit University

After over a decade of healing crusades, in 1959, Roberts felt a shift was coming that would help him multiply his ministry by training up young people to take the healing message to the world. In June 1960, Roberts announced to his partners a plan to start a "soul-winning training program" to increase his overseas evangelistic ministry.[28] During a crusade in Norfolk, Virginia in 1961, he was having dinner with Pat Robertson, the Charismatic evangelist and founder of the Christian Broadcast Network, when God spoke these words to Roberts:

> Raise up your students to hear my voice, to go where My light is dim, where My voice is heard small and where My healing power is not known. To go to the uttermost bounds of the earth. Their work will exceed yours and in this I am well pleased.[29]

This message reminded Roberts of what God said to him on his deathbed at seventeen years old: "Son, I am going to heal you and you are going to take my

---

[27] Harrell, *Oral Roberts*, 306.
[28] Oral Roberts, "God has Spoken to me Again," *Abundant Life*, June 1960, 6-9.
[29] Roberts, *Expect a Miracle*, 162.

healing power to your generation. You are to build me a university and built it upon My authority and upon the Holy Spirit."[30] With this fresh vision, a new era began for Roberts' ministry.

In May of 1962, the vision for a university became clearer as Roberts announced the construction of a new building in south Tulsa to house not simply a soul-winning program, as was previously announced, but a university. Roberts told his partners,

> To further fulfill God's call upon my life to take His healing power to my generation, I feel the time has come to undertake by faith the greatest and most far-reaching step of all for the salvation of souls and to perpetuate this ministry that God has given me and committed to my trust. That is to build the ORAL ROBERTS UNIVERSITY OF EVANGELISM.[31]

The task of building a university from the ground up was overwhelming to Roberts. Once again he had to draw upon the resources he had in the Holy Spirit to lead the way. The only thing he knew to do was to walk the barren acres of the plot of land at 81st and Lewis and pray in the Spirit. Roberts recalls, "I was literally groaning and praying and crying out, 'Oh God, help me! Show me the way!'"[32] Each time the Spirit would well up in him, he would pray in tongues and ask God for the interpretation. This process was exhilarating for Roberts and gave him a hunger to regularly pray in this manner.[33] As he received the interpretation of his prayers, he testified, "the Lord revealed to me the most astonishing knowledge and showed me the broad outline of how to build a university." [34] Roberts employed Cecil Stanfield to design the new facilities. The first buildings were the Timko Barton building and the two residence halls named after Lee Braxton and Demos Shakarian, which formed a U-shape campus. They contained space for hosting conferences, classrooms and house those who would attend the "University of Evangelism."

---

[30] ibid., 158.
[31] Oral Roberts, "A Spiritual Revolution Throughout the Earth," *Abundant Life*, May 1962, 6-10.
[32] Roberts, *Expect a Miracle*, 173.
[33] Oral Roberts, *Unleashing the Power of Praying in the Spirit* (Tulsa, OK: Harrison House, 1993), 46.
[34] Roberts, *Expect a Miracle*, 174.

To open the new University, Roberts hosted week-long Ministers Seminars devoted to the topic of the Holy Spirit and the gifts of the Holy Spirit that were attended by more than 350 ministers from eleven denominations.[35] Roberts knew that ORU would be an important place for uniting the Pentecostal and Charismatic movement. He also established a special research library, The Pentecostal Research Center, to collect and archive materials from Pentecostal and Charismatic bodies all over the world. Roberts wanted ORU to be the best place to study the Holy Spirit. Today, the center is called the Holy Spirit Research Center.

ORU is known for its unique mid-century modernistic architecture. Frank Wallace designed the futuristic feel of the new academic buildings to match Roberts' positive message of faith and his belief that "all things were possible."[36] The optimism of the new buildings sent a clear message that ORU was going to be a place of possibility and miracles. One of the most iconic structures on the campus is the Prayer Tower. According to Roberts, God instructed him to put it in the center of campus to represent that the Spirit would be the "center of the University."[37] The two-hundred-foot, futuristic, cross-shaped design is crowned with an "eternal flame" symbolizing the baptism in the Holy Spirit.[38] The dramatic height of the tower serves as a constant reminder that ORU was built on prayer, particularly the practice of praying in tongues with interpretation. The tower also houses an "upper room" designed to introduce a new generation to the power of the Spirit. From the top to the bottom, ORU would be "built on the Holy Spirit."[39]

---

[35] "ORU School of Evangelism Opens," *Abundant Life,* April 1963, 1.

[36] For more on ORU architecture, see my blog "The Architectural Inspiration of Oral Roberts University," October 14, 2020, https://danieldisgrigg.com/2020/10/14/oruarchitecture/

[37] Roberts, *Unleashing the Power of Praying in the Spirit*, 87.

[38] Oral Roberts, "Why Build A Prayer Tower," *Oral Roberts University Outreach* 3, no. 1 (Winter 1966): 7-10. Early architectural drawings of the Prayer Tower were designed with more of a space age crown design. But by 1966, the concept had been morphed to that of a "20th Century cross, one that challenges the youth of a nuclear space age" to place an importance on prayer. The tower was slender to portray the "inner man of the person standing on the inside." The height of the tower was designed to inspire man to "reach toward God." Included with the tower was a series of "prayer gardens." (8).

[39] According to Roberts in "My Eighteen Hours with God in Miami, Florida," *Abundant Life* 17, no. 5 (May 1963): 7, "One of the buildings on the University campus will be the Abundant Life

9.5 1967 ORU Dedication Day (Copyright, Oral Roberts University)

Oral Roberts' vision of "whole person" education emphasized the development of the spirit-mind-body together. It was a unique concept in higher education at the time. Equally innovative was his vision for technology in learning. The Learning Resources Center had a state of the art "Dial Access Retrieval System" in which students could access lectures and other media anywhere across campus. When ORU was officially dedicated in 1967, Oral Roberts invited Evangelist Billy Graham to be the keynote speaker. It was clear that ORU was situating itself to becoming one of the premier Christian universities in the nation.

Roberts Becomes a Methodist

On May 25, 1968, Oral Roberts made an announcement that shocked the Pentecostal community. He was going to join the Methodist Church. Having maintained his credentials with the Pentecostal Holiness Church for over thirty years, the ecumenical expansion of his ministry had reached a point that transcended its Pentecostal base to include a broad range of denominations. Roberts' influence on the new Charismatic Renewal had placed him in a position

Prayer Tower which will rise over 100 feet above the ground, with cloven tongues of fire burning perpetually at its top, symbolizing our complete dependence upon the Holy Spirit. It will house our prayer group as well as provide an 'upper room' for prayer and meditation by both students and visitors. We expect many to receive the Holy Spirit in this upper room."

in which mainline Charismatics saw him as a spiritual father.[40] The decision was made with surprisingly little fanfare in the media and his own publications and Roberts assured the ORU community that,

> [t]hey have said... we need a strong Pentecostal infusion and you epitomize this in the world. And we urgently and desperately need this outpouring within our movement... I am Pentecostal and will be until the day I die.[41]

Oral and Evelyn Roberts made Boston Avenue United Methodist Church their new church home and became close friends with the pastor, Finis Crutchfield. His primary motivation in joining the Methodist Church was to expand his ministry of healing and the power of the Spirit to the broader mainline church. Although the move was ultimately detrimental to Roberts' support base, he believed it fulfilled God's call to bring healing power to his generation.[42] This decision was crucial for Roberts' growing influence on the Charismatic Renewal. ORU broadened its reach by expanding beyond just Pentecostals to appeal to Spirit-filled believers from a number of mainline Protestant and Catholic circles. ORU affiliated the seminary as a Methodist Seminary and invited Dr. James Buskirk to be the Dean. Roberts' affiliation with the Methodist Church remained until the mid-1980s.

City of Faith

The controversial decision to build the City of Faith hospital and research center in 1981 would deal a terrible blow to Roberts' reputation. Once a favorite son, his attempts to build a hospital put him at odds with city officials. Then, his efforts to raise funds to build the hospital debt free and fully fund scholarships for the medical students became a point of national ridicule. His Methodist financial base abandoned him and the American public turned on him.

Until this time, despite their similar Pentecostal origins and close proximity, Roberts and Kenneth Hagin, the leader of the Word of Faith Movement, did not

---

[40] Synan, "Oral Roberts: Son of Pentecostalism, Father of the Charismatic Movement," 5-21.

[41] Oral Roberts, "My Decision to Enter the Methodist Denomination," Faculty Meeting, Oral Roberts University (March 15, 1968); Digital Showcase (Oral Roberts University) http://digitalshowcase.oru.edu/oruav/7/.

[42] Harrell, *Oral Roberts*, 297-99.

have a close association. Yet during this period, Hagin stepped into this vacuum to support Roberts, who became characterized as a prosperity teacher.[43]

Despite those difficult years, ORU has endured as a pillar of the Tulsa community and continued to produce quality graduates who have been in demand by Tulsa industries. In 2007, a new chapter in its story began when the David Green family of Hobby Lobby fame partnered with the university to stabilize the financial situation. Under new board chair, Mart Green, ORU implemented new governance and welcomed Mark Rutland as the new president who led the much-needed campus revitalization and ethos of the university until 2013.[44] Under the leadership of the current president, Dr. William M. Wilson, ORU has experienced unprecedented growth through globalization. Wilson has emerged as a global leader in the Spirit-empowered movement as Co-Chair of Empowered21 and chair of the Pentecostal World Fellowship. He has led capital campaigns for new buildings including the award-winning Global Learning Center, track and tennis facilities, nursing and engineering buildings, and the first new residential building since 1976. Today, the university is debt free and has re-established itself as a leading university in the global Spirit-empowered Movement.

Racial Equality

In the 1960s and 1970s ORU was one of the few places in Tulsa where racial integration was intentional. Throughout Roberts' ministry, his integrated meetings showed his belief that people were just people, no matter their skin color. But when he transitioned to the university in the 1960s, his inclusion turned to intentional activism. While it is unclear what Roberts knew of the city's racial history, his legacy as a pioneer in racial integration in the Pentecostal community made him welcome among blacks in Tulsa.[45] In 1968, when several of Tulsa's black business leaders went to New York to solicit help establishing new businesses in North Tulsa, the

---

[43] To understand more about the controversy of the City of Faith and Roberts place in prosperity gospel, see Isgrigg, "'I Tried Poverty,'" 5-24.

[44] Neil Eskelin, *The New ORU: Empowered for the 21st Century* (Tulsa, OK: Oral Roberts University). https://digitalshowcase.oru.edu/oru_books/1/

[45] Isgrigg, "Healing for All Races," 227-56.

powerbrokers told them, "Call Oral Roberts. He is the one man in Tulsa who can help you."[46] After meeting with them and listening to the injustices they had experienced from banks in Tulsa, he commented, "The white man's oppression of blacks is one of the most sordid chapters in American's history—and oppression is still going on… I want to help. I will call on as many friends as I have here in Tulsa to try to help." Roberts admonished them to see God ultimately as their source.

Oral Roberts University was Roberts' greatest contribution to promoting racial equality in Tulsa.[47] When it came to integration, ORU was ahead of the curve for conservative evangelical universities because Roberts wanted more from his university than to simply produce good Christian men and women. He dreamed of a university where students had equal opportunities to succeed regardless of racial or social background. When a federal governmental official funding asked his policy on integration, Roberts replied, "Well, let me give you the bigger policy. ORU is established in three ways. First, to be international. Second to be interdenominational. And third to be interracial."[48] ORU's interracial admissions policy was in place before government affirmative action policies and the 1978 Supreme Court decision permitted race to be a factor.

Roberts believed that part of ORU's mission would be to prove to America that "no black person is inferior." He declared, "We have demonstrated to our constituency and our city what is so obvious all along if you had eyes to see. We are the same people. All we need is the same opportunity. Give us the same opportunity, folks and I am telling you, there is no color."[49] In the 1970s, troubled that whites in south Tulsa were discriminating against blacks and would not rent apartments to blacks, Roberts raised money to buy a local complex so black

---

[46] Oral Roberts, *The Call: Oral Roberts Autobiography* (New York: Avon Books, 1971), 108-109.

[47] See Isgrigg, "Healing for all Races: Oral Roberts' Legacy of Racial Reconciliation in a Divided City," 227-56.

[48] Oral Roberts, "God Doesn't Look at Skin Color," ORU Chapel, September 26, 1989, Digital Showcase (Oral Roberts University), accessed December 21, 2020, https://digitalshowcase.oru.edu/cgi/viewcontent.cgi?article=1008&context=chapel.

[49] Oral Roberts, "Oral Roberts Meets with Bishops," audio cassette, Holy Spirit Research Center, Oral Roberts University, Tulsa, OK, August 31, 1989. https://digitalshowcase.oru.edu/oruav/13

students could have equal access.[50] To further make his point, he appointed Clifton Taulbert, a notable black alumnus who had also been rejected for an apartment because of his race, as an administrator of one of ORU's housing complexes. Taulbert went on to become a notable Tulsa community leader as an entrepreneur and Pulitzer Prize nominated author of the best-selling books, *Eight Habits of the Heart*, *Last Train North*, and *Once Upon a Time When We Were Colored*.

Roberts also encouraged white students to listen to the voices from the black community. In 1972 as part of a yearly "Black Awareness Week," Roberts held a panel of black Tulsa leaders who discussed racism, poverty, and black-white relations.[51] One panelist, Don Ross, an outspoken advocate for North Tulsa, later served as a representative in the Oklahoma House from 1983–2000. Ross, a journalist-turned-politician, spent more than four decades trying to summon the Race Massacre event from history by publishing several articles in the *Oklahoma Eagle*. In the 1960s his advocacy for blacks Tulsan resulted in establishing the 1921 Race Riot Commission. Riot historian, James Hirsch, commented, "No one played a more crucial role in this endeavor than Don Ross."[52]

In February 2018, ORU President Wilson, announced proudly, "For the first time in ORU history, white students are in the minority."[53] His announcement came as no surprise to those who have watched ORU become a bright spot of diversity in Tulsa. In 2018, ORU's student body was 45 percent white, 14 percent African American, 14 percent Hispanic, and 16 percent international students representing 105 countries.[54] Under Clarence Boyd, an African American who has served many years as Vice President of Student Affairs, the black heritage emphasis has expanded to several celebrations hosted by the student Multi-cultural

---

[50] Oral Roberts and Larry Lea, "Going Beyond Reconciliation to Restitution," *Kingdom Lifeline*, January/February 1987, 9.

[51] "Black Awareness Chapel," ORU Chapel Transcript, February 16, 1972, accessed December 28, 2018, Digital Showcase (Oral Roberts University) https://digitalshowcase.oru.edu/chapel/6/.

[52] Hirsch, *Riot and Remembrance*, 187.

[53] William M. Wilson, ORU Chapel, February 7, 2018, Oral Roberts University, Tulsa, Oklahoma.

[54] "Quick Facts 2018: Enrollment at Census Date," Oral Roberts University Registrar's Office, Oral Roberts University, Tulsa, Oklahoma.

Committee, including "MLK and Diversity Week," "International Emphasis Week," and an annual "CultureFest."[55] While the city has continued to struggle with integration, ORU serves as a model for diversity and an example of Christ's ability to bring racial healing.

T. L. and Daisy Osborn

Another important mid-century evangelist, Tommy Lee Osborn, was born in 1923 in Skedee, north and west of Tulsa near Pawnee.[56] His Baptist father came from Missouri to minister in Oklahoma Territory. One of thirteen children, Osborn grew up in poverty until a rich man in Tulsa invited his father to run a three-thousand-acre ranch.

T. L. was introduced to Pentecostalism when his brother, Lonnie, attended a "holy roller" meeting in a brush arbor in Mannford, a few miles south and east of Skedee.[57] The twelve year old accompanied him to the revival led by Dulcie Hoffman where he surrendered his life to Jesus, was baptized in the Holy Spirit, and sensed a call on his life to ministry.

After his conversion, Osborn attended a Pentecostal church in a small oil-field town of Naval Reserve, near Skedee. There his pastor, Ernest M. Dillard, took interest in him and asked him to play his accordion in his revival meetings. It wasn't long before Dillard asked him to preach during his revivals. In 1939, at age sixteen, Osborn traveled full-time with Dillard and was ordained in the Pentecostal Church of God. That year, he met Oral Roberts who was holding a revival at the Sand Springs Pentecostal Holiness Church.[58] Osborn teamed with Roberts to hold street crusades. Roberts stayed for the next few months to lead the church. This would be the beginning a lifelong friendship.

In 1940, Osborn traveled with Dillard to revival meetings. At one meeting in Los Banos, California, he met his future wife, Daisy Marie Washburn, and knew

---

[55] Clarence Boyd, "Historical Account of the Multi-Cultural Committee," n.d., Office of Student Affairs, Oral Roberts University, Tulsa, Oklahoma.

[56] Edith Prakash, *Yesterday, Today, and Forever: The Extraordinary Life and Ministry of Tommy Lee Osborn* (Lanham, MD: Seymour Press, 2018), 35-38.

[57] Osborn, *Faith Library*, 36-37.

[58] "To Conduct a Revival," *Sand Springs Leader*, April 6, 1939, 3.

instantly they would be married. Daisy was born in Merced, California September 23, 1924. She and her ten siblings were raised on a farm until her mother died in an accident when she was eight years old. Daisy went to live with an older sister and was active in her Assemblies of God church. At twelve, she gave her life to Christ. When a missionary to India visited the church, she gave her an Indian sari and told her she would become a missionary. Gerald Roberts married them on April 5, 1942 at the Los Banos Full Gospel Church. The next day, the couple moved to Sand Springs, where they prepared to minister and itinerate for the mission field.[59]

In 1946, the Osborns went as missionaries in India, but the situation that did not go well. After ten months of frustrated ministry, they returned to the states in McMinnville, Oregon to pastor a Full Gospel Church.[60] Later, Osborn attended a William Branham healing service when he became interested in healing ministry.

Osborn pioneered the idea of "healing en masse" after one of his mentors, F. F. Bosworth, challenged him with the idea that if salvation could be prayed for en masse, why not healing?[61] After prayer and fasting, the Holy Spirit spoke to him and said, "My son, as I was with [Charles] Price, [Smith] Wigglesworth, and others, so I will be with thee. They are dead, but now it is time for you to arise, to go, and do likewise." [62] Osborn was also challenged by a sermon by evangelist, Hattie Hammond, who preached, "If you ever see Jesus, you will never be the same again." Shortly after, T. L. and Daisy had an experience of Jesus walking into their room while they were praying. This revelation of the reality of Jesus transformed their ministry and gave them the faith to believe that when they ministered to the sick, Jesus was there with them.

In 1949, the Osborns settled in Tulsa, where they established their first ministry headquarters at 1029 N. Utica. They renovated the two-story building to house

---

[59] Osborn, *Faith Library*, vol. 1, 347-49.
[60] T. L. Osborn, "My Life Story and Call to the Healing Ministry," *The Voice of Healing*, September 1949, 6.
[61] Daniel King and Daniel D. Isgrigg, "Healing En Masse," a paper presented at the Empowered21 Scholars Consultation, Tulsa, Oklahoma, June 2020, 4.
[62] Osborn, "My Life Story and Call to the Healing Ministry," 5.

their "Voice of Faith" ministry. Osborn published *Faith Digest*, where he told of the miracles that were taking place in his healing ministry. They also set out to take this healing message on the mission field, especially in Africa. In 1953, Osborn introduced the idea of "native evangelism," the methodology of preaching in large campaigns, but leaving native pastors and leaders to organize and minister to those who received Christ.[63]

In 1962, as they continued to hold crusades around the world, the Osborns began working on a new facility near 1400 E. Skelly near 51st and Lewis—the 180,000-square-foot facility to house the worldwide ministry, a missionary training school, and missions museum. In the 1980s, T. L. and Daisy became greatly influential in teaching ministry in independent and Word of Faith circles.

The Osborns were particularly recognized for lifting up the ministry of women in the church. Their egalitarian message was reflective of not only Daisy's vital ministry, but the New Testament's elevation of women. T. L. and Daisy truly were equals in their life and their ministry. Their ministry has continued on through their daughter, Dr. Ladonna Osborn who serves as president and CEO of Osborn Ministries International, pastor of International Gospel Center, and founder of International Gospel Fellowship, a global network of 1,000 churches. She is also Co-Founder and President of the Women's International Network which encourages, educates, and equips women for all areas of Christian ministry.

Kenneth E. Hagin and Rhema Bible Church

One of the most iconic scenes in the Tulsa suburb of Broken Arrow, is a large church that features a shield with the word "Faith" on the pinnacle of its roof. In Charismatic circles, Kenneth Hagin's legacy is synonymous with the concept of faith. Others before him talked about faith, but as Kate Bowler notes, "Faith was seen as an absolute law, and as such it operated as a universal and uniform reality; there need not be a leap of faith, as faith would prove itself."[64] Hagin emphasized

---

[63] Harrell, *All Things Are Possible*, 65.
[64] Kate Bowler, *Blessed: A History of the American Prosperity Gospel* (New York: Oxford University Press, 2013), 46.

positive confession as a way of accessing God's blessings. His teachings on faith were so influential that his followers and disciples have become a highly visible stream of Charismatic Christianity called the Word of Faith Movement.

Hagin was born August 20, 1917, in McKinney, Texas. Premature and weighing only two pounds, the doctors initially believed he was still born. But a nurse detected a heartbeat and cared for the two-pound baby until he was strong enough to go home. His early years were filled with sickness and by age fifteen, he had serious heart problems and became bedfast. All the doctors gave up on him. Partially paralyzed, Hagin turned to the Bible for comfort and was particularly drawn to the words of healing. One day, Hagin discovered Mark 11:23-24. The words about speaking and believing ignited his heart. He confessed healing over his body. On August 8, 1934, Hagin received his healing. He launched into a preaching ministry at the age of seventeen.

In April 1937, Hagin received the baptism in the Holy Ghost at a full gospel church. There he met Earl J. Rogers, who invited him to join him in holding a meeting in Roland, Texas. Hagin preached with great success and then accepted a call to pastor a full gospel church in Tom Bean, Texas. It was there that he met his wife, Lois Oretha Rooker, and they were married on November 25, 1938. For the next two decades, Hagin pastored full gospel churches in Texas, preaching the typical Pentecostal message but with particular emphasis on healing and faith.

In May 1950, Hagin had an experience that would forever shape his place in the Pentecostal and Charismatic community. During a time of prayer, God spoke to him and said, "Go teach My people faith!"[65] From that time on, faith became a centerpiece of his messages. Fully embracing Pentecost and the baptism in the Holy Spirit, Hagin was also strongly used in prophetic ministry that accompanied his preaching. By the mid-1950s, he was a regular speaker at the Full Gospel Businessmen's Fellowship conventions.

In 1966, Hagin was encouraged to move to Tulsa by several friends in the Full Gospel Businessmen's Fellowship. One of those friends, Lee Eller, showed him the office building T. L. Osborn's ministry had just vacated at 1029 N. Utica. They

---

[65] A good portion of this narrative was drawn from information in *Kenneth E. Hagin's 50 Years in the Ministry (1934–1984)* (Broken Arrow, OK: Rhema Bible Church, 1984).

bought the building, and Hagin's daughter and son-in-law, Pat and Buddy Harrison, moved into the upstairs. Hagin began holding "Faith Seminars" and continued traveling to speak at Full Gospel Businessmen's Fellowship conventions around the country. He also began publishing his *The Word of Faith* magazine, and started his "Voice of Faith" radio broadcast where he mixed his classical messages of the Holy Spirit with a new emphasis on faith.

In 1973, Hagin began a new yearly campmeeting in Tulsa. The first was held at Sheridan Christian Center and included Hagin, Roy Hicks, J. R. Goodwin, and Vicki Jamieson. The campmeeting drew people from around the U.S. and accelerated his popularity. A year later, he decided to build a training center to host his conferences and campmeetings. By 1975, crowds for the campmeeting of nearly 5,000 packed the Tulsa Convention Center. Hagin taught his increasingly popular messages on faith rooted in the verse he had heard when he was healed as a boy—Mark 11:23.

In December 1974, the vision for a training center became clearer when God spoke to Hagin again. He recalls,

> I saw it in the Spirit—that He wants us to have right here in Tulsa a healing—a prayer—no, put prayer first—a prayer and healing center where people can come … We'll go out to some of them, but some of them need to come and stay until they do get healed.[66]

In May 1975, the first class of Rhema Bible Training Center included fifty-eight students who met at Sheridan Christian Center. The training center was designed to be a two-year Bible school and boot camp for ministry led by his son, Kenneth, Jr. Meanwhile, a new facility for Bible School and Church was being built in Broken Arrow. It opened April 17, 1977.[67]

The story of the property on which Rhema was built goes back to around 1908, when Pentecost first came to Broken Arrow. In a revival under Willard Pope, a young man named Rupert Bailey was filled with the Holy Spirit. Following that experience, Rupert prayed all day for the salvation of souls while he worked on his

---

[66] "Winter Bible Seminar Hotels: Take a Tour of the Rhema Campus," Kenneth Hagin Ministries, accessed 21 October 2020, https://www.rhema.org/index.php?option=com_content&view=category&id=174&Itemid=132.

[67] *Kenneth E. Hagin's 50 Years in the Ministry*, 74-83.

parent's farm. One day he had a vision that a mighty soul winning ministry would be birthed from that property. He did not know that seventy years later, Rhema Bible Training Center would train up men and women in the gospel and send them around the world.[68] Today the campus houses ten buildings, including the church, classroom facilities, student housing, a recreation center, administrative building, and a beautiful wooded park that hosts an annual Christmas light display with over two million lights.

With Hagin joining Roberts and Osborn, Tulsa became recognized as a capital of Charismatic ministries. Hagin and Roberts became close friends in the early 1980s. In 1979, in the midst of Roberts' declining support and greatest fundraising demands, Hagin invited him to his annual campmeeting in Tulsa. During one of the services, Hagin shared his deep appreciation for Roberts and surprised him by taking a love offering to help him with his vision.[69] That night, Hagin, Kenneth Copeland, John Osteen, and Pat and Debbie Boone led the way as the audience overflowed with pledges to save the City of Faith. This gesture deeply moved Roberts, who commented that, "I sat with my head in my hands, tears flowing down my cheeks, realizing that nothing like this had ever happened on my behalf."[70] In 1983, Roberts, Hagin, and Osborn ministered together—the first time they had all shared the same stage.[71]

---

[68] "Winter Bible Seminar Hotels."

[69] Harrell, *Oral Roberts*, 424.

[70] Oral Roberts, "The Night I Found Out That God Hadn't Forgotten Me in My Struggle," *Abundant Life*, October 1979, 6-13.

[71] See Isgrigg, "'I Tried Poverty'," 16-17.

9.5 – Osborn, Hagin, and Roberts at a 1983 Hagin Campmeeting (HSRC)

Hagin died September 19, 2003, following nearly seventy years of ministry. His message of faith was highly influential in creating a new segment of the Pentecostal and Charismatic tradition called the "Word of Faith" movement. Many independent Charismatic ministers have followed in his message of faith, including Kenneth Copeland, Fred Price, Charles Capps, Keith Moore, and others.

Carlton Pearson & Higher Dimensions

Perhaps the most impactful black Pentecostal pastor and church in Tulsa in recent years is Carlton Pearson and Higher Dimensions Evangelistic Center. Although currently an outcast of the evangelical community due to his controversial shift to the "gospel of inclusion," Pearson became a significant figure in Pentecostal and Charismatic circles in the 1980s-1990s. He grew up in a poor neighborhood in San Diego, California, where his family attended the Church of God in Christ under Bishop J. E. Blake. He and his mother also watched Roberts on television. Pearson was called to preach at an early age and hoped he could attend ORU after high school, because there were no black Pentecostal universities.[72]

---

[72] "I'm On My Way to Becoming a World Changer," *Abundant Life*, September 1972, 16.

When he arrived at ORU in 1971, Roberts almost immediately recognized Pearson's gifts and believed he was special. Within a year, Pearson was one of the most recognized black students on campus. In 1973, Roberts shared with Pearson an idea that would change his outlook on his own ethnicity. He said, "Carlton, the last person to help Christ on earth was a black man." Roberts added, "I believe that the next great move of the Holy Spirit would be among black people... And that you will have a leading part in it."[73] That year Pearson was the driving force behind instituting the "Black Awareness Week" and was regularly called upon to encourage black participation in campus life. He and Timothy Thuston started an all-black choir on campus called "Souls-A-Fire" and he was a regular singer with the ORU World Action Singers featured on Roberts' prime time specials. After graduation, Pearson was appointed "Associate Evangelist" and chaplain for Oral Roberts Ministries, and he ministered side by side with Richard Roberts at crusades around the world. Pearson's relationship with Oral was close, and he claims that in 1974 Oral singled him out as his "black son."[74]

After a few years of ministry success under Roberts' wing, in April 1977, Pearson launched out on his own evangelistic ministry, singing and preaching in churches around the country. In 1982, he launched Higher Dimensions Family Church an interracial church located in the suburb of Jenks, on Main Street, west of Elm Street, with his friend Gary MacIntosh.[75] They also started a ministry training school focused on training people in prayer, worship, study of God's Word, and the Holy Spirit. The church was integrated, but that was primarily achieved because it was it was planted in South Tulsa rather than North Tulsa. Pearson's success in bridging the black-white division as well as his ecumenical appeal helped grow his church to over 10,000 people. They purchased a large church building at 86th Street and S. Memorial Drive, originally built by Bob Yandian and Grace

---

[73] Carlton D. Pearson, "Oral Roberts' Prophetic Word at Azusa 1996 with Carlton Pearson," accessed December 31, 2018, https://youtu.be/vdXRuVaLkFU.

[74] "Hell and High Water," *Reform*, May 2013, 15

[75] D. J. Hedges, "Pearson, Carlton Demetrius," Stanley M. Burgess and Eduard Van der Mass, eds., *New International Dictionary of Pentecostal and Charismatic Movements* (Nashville, TN: Zondervan, 2002), 960.

Fellowship. Part of Pearson's success was that he represented a version of blackness that whites would accept because he was not "too black."[76]

Pearson's notoriety in Pentecostal and Charismatic circles, interracial leadership, visibility in Christian media, and economic wealth allowed black spirituality to become mainstream. As Marla Frederick points out, Pearson represented a new face of Black Pentecostalism by "aesthetically affirming black uplift and social mobility."[77] Pearson's popularity led to him being invited to be the first African American host of TBN's "Praise the Lord" television show. He used his success to provide opportunities for other Black ministers to achieve similar visibility and break economic barriers. On the one hand, Pearson embraced his African American identity, while at the same time, was critical of his own community focusing too much on being black. On the other hand, Pearson was uncomfortable with the way white ministers used popular black preachers like himself to only address racial integration in the church. He wanted to be recognized as minister, not a token black preacher for white audiences. Pearson comments, "they needed me as an evangelist before the blacks came, because my ministry is just as effective to a nonblack audience as an integrated audience."[78]

In 1988, one of Pearson's most significant efforts was his establishment of the Azusa Conferences, which became a platform for a new wave of black ministers to be noticed by the larger church community in the early 1990s. Most notable among them was T. D. Jakes, the mega church pastor who became a household name as America's favorite preacher. [79] Others, like Donnie McClurkin, Dion Sanders, and Marvin Winans, were elevated to visibility through their presence on predominantly white Christian television. Beside, many of the COGIC's favorite preachers and singers were given a platform previously unknown to Black Pentecostalism by being showcased live on Trinity Broadcast Network. In this way, Pearson was able to "legitimize" black Pentecostal spirituality to white audiences.[80]

---

[76] Fredrick, *Colored Television*, 47.

[77] Marla F. Fredrick, *Colored Television: American Religion Gone Global* (Palo Alto: Stanford University Press, 2015), 36.

[78] "Interview with Carlton Pearson," *Bridgebuilder* March/April 1987, 11-12.

[79] Shayne Lee, *T.D. Jakes: America's New Preacher* (New York: New York University Press, 2005).

[80] Fredrick, *Colored Television*, 49.

He used the conferences to start the Azusa Fellowship, a ministerial fellowship of over 400 ministries and ministers.

In 2001, Pearson ran for mayor of Tulsa. He unsuccessfully campaigned as a conservative black Republican hoping to build unity in issues such as race relations, education and economic development particularly in the African American community.[81]

In the early 2000s, Pearson took a controversial turn by embracing universalism. This caused a major fallout between him and most of the rest of the Pentecostal and Charismatic community, including Oral Roberts. By 2003, his church started to dwindle. The next year the Joint College of African-American Pentecostal Bishops denounced his heretical views. In 2008, he closed his church and his remaining followers merged with All Souls Unitarian Church, where he regularly preaches his new thought metaphysical gospel infused with Pentecostal motifs. In 2018, the story of Pearson's life was featured in the Netflix documentary movie, *Come Sunday*.

---

[81] P. J. Lassick, "Carlton Pearson To Run for Mayor," *Tulsa World*, October 31, 2001, https://tulsaworld.com/archive/carlton-pearson-to-run-for-mayor/article_c45f18ed-0a0e-5e79-8e2f-9a4f6dd1e1fe.html (accessed 17 February 2021).

10

KNOWING THE PAST, EMBRACING THE FUTURE

It has been said that Tulsa has excelled in two primary industries: oil and Jesus. The story of Pentecostals in Tulsa has proven this true. Oil provided wealth and opportunities for Tulsa's citizens, but its churches have been essential to the fabric of the community. They have provided stability and quality of life for Tulsa's religious citizens. It is a rich legacy of Christian faith that goes back as far as the beginnings of this metropolitan city. The Pentecostal story is but one of many stories of Christian churches where revival fires helped fuel the growth of significant congregations. Its pastors have served at the highest levels of Pentecostal denominations and it has been the headquarters of major international ministries. The wealth of the city contributed to the success of the churches and funded the work of the gospel for many generations. These factors made Tulsa a favored destination for pastors and new ministries.

Tulsa has also been a place where ordinary people can be raised up to do great things. Tulsa helped poor Pentecostal ministers, like Oral Roberts and Kenneth Hagin, become household names. Many other unlikely heroes rose from obscurity to places of leadership and significance in this town. This is illustrated in the significant role women played in origins of Pentecostalism in Tulsa. Tulsa's story would be quite different without Vandella Frye, who brought Pentecostalism to Tulsa in 1908 and led the Apostolic Faith Mission until 1912, or the three Church Mothers who established the First Church of God in Christ in 1914. Where would Tulsa be without Aimee Semple McPherson, whose 1918 and 1919 campaigns were instrumental in building the church in Tulsa? Not to mention the large legacy of Mattie McCaulley, Mattie McGlothen, and Minnie Black. Women, such as Ada Lois Sipuel Fisher, pushed the boundaries of what is possible for African Americans in Oklahoma and played a role in the Civil Rights Movement. Tulsa benefitted greatly from the Pentecostal ethos that empowers women to preach and to lead, even though some denominations did not let women serve as pastors.

Tulsa is also a story of revivals. There have been significant moments in Tulsa's history when believers gathered together, and God showed up in mighty ways. These revivals built churches and changed people's lives. They encouraged the faithful, raised people up from sick beds, and gave hope to the hurting. We study the past to know what God has done so we can know what is possible today. Tulsa has a future because the God Pentecostals proclaim is the same "yesterday, today, and forever." The methods may have changed over the past century, but every generation deserves an opportunity to experience Pentecost for themselves. For this to be possible, the Spirit-empowered church in Tulsa must introduce a new generation to the power of the Spirit and the God of miracles. Just like the past, this is the key to reviving existing churches and establishing new works that will impact the generations to come.

Yet Tulsa has essentially two Pentecostal communities—one white and one black. One hundred years after the Race Massacre, the two communities rarely mix and are still geographically separate. This racial legacy is, at least in part, the result of the Massacre and the racial attitudes of this city. The perpetual flight of white Pentecostal churches to the suburbs has continued to separate white and black citizens and reinforced the distance between the communities. This distance is a barrier to racial empathy and hindered true unity. Even today, the issues that face African Americans in North Tulsa—food deserts, inadequate housing, inequity in education, racism, and lack of job opportunities—are rarely addressed by white Pentecostal Churches. Too often, when racial issues happen in Tulsa, the white community repeats the sins of 1921 by failing to recognize black pain and suffering and leaving their brothers and sisters to grieve alone.

Pentecost is a vision of what could be if the Holy Spirit is allowed to heal the church. The good news is that since 1921, healing and reconciliation has been taking place. Survivors like Otis Clark used the Pentecostal message to build bridges and uphold the values early Pentecostals exhibited. The Apostle Peter confirmed the prophesy of Joel, "In the last days, I will pour out my spirit on all flesh" (Acts 2:17). The promise of Pentecost unites us as one body, baptized into one Spirit, is the only thing that can recapture the original vision of the Azusa Street Mission. Our shared story is an opportunity for white and black believers begin to honor one another by seeing each other through the Spirit's eyes as one community. When we do this, we can find the commonality that will build bridges.

Why did Tulsa become the home of so many significant ministries? While reflecting on the findings of this research, ORU president, Billy Wilson, shared that he believes God chose Tulsa because perhaps no other American community needed the message of healing more. From Native Americans losing their lands to white settlers to the tragedy of the Massacre and its after effects, Tulsa has been a deeply broken community that only God's message of healing can heal. Because of this, God sent Aimee Semple McPherson during a pandemic and Raymond T. Richey after the Massacre. Then again, in anticipation of the Civil Rights Movement, he moved J. L. Alaman to Tulsa to hold interracial meetings and Oral Roberts to promote racial inclusion and healing. From Tulsa, God's message of healing went out and impacted the whole world.

Hopefully, this story will contribute to the healing Tulsa wounds. Without denying the past, we can lean into a more just future in which we see ourselves as one body. The progress of the past few decades has opened new opportunities for black voices speak and the white community to begin to listen. The building and rebuilding of Greenwood demonstrated what African Americans can do if given the space to lead, excel, and prosper without barriers of injustice.

By neglecting the black Pentecostal story, white Tulsans have robbed themselves of the rich the gifts this community has to offer us. If we can understand that the same Spirit who created the prosperity of Greenwood is the Spirit of Pentecost, where all flesh has equal access to all of God's fullness. For Tulsa's fullest success can only be achieved when its black citizens share in its prosperity.

I believe the Holy Spirit is drawing us into a future where the power of the Spirit will help us know and care about one another. Black and white Pentecostal churches must see ourselves as one family—one Tulsa, not north and south, and one Church—not black or white. Join me in praying that the next century we will see that kind of "Pentecost in Tulsa."

BIBLIOGRAPHY

Pentecostal, Tulsa, and Oklahoma History

Alexander, Estrelda. *Black Fire: One Hundred Years of African American Pentecostalism.* Downers Grove: IVP Academic, 2011.

Alexander Estrelda Y., ed. *Dictionary of Pan-African Pentecostalism* vol 1. Eugene, OR: Wipf & Stock, 2019.

Alexander, Paul. *Peace to War: Shifting Allegiances in the Assemblies of God.* Telfor, PA: Cascadia Publishing House, 2009.

Bean, Bobby. *This is the Church of God in Christ.* Atlanta: Underground Epics Pub., 2001.

Blumhofer, Edith L. "William H. Durham: Years of Creativity, Years of Dissent." In *Portraits of a Generation*, edited by James R. Goff Jr. and Grant Wacker, 123-43. Fayetteville, AR: University of Arkansas Press, 2002.

Bond, O. H. *Life Story of O. H. Bond.* Oakgrove, AR: n.p., n.d.

Bowler, Kate. *Blessed: A History of the American Prosperity Gospel.* New York: Oxford University Press, 2013.

Brumback, Carl. *Like a River.* Springfield, MO: Gospel Publishing House, 1977.

———. *Suddenly...From Heaven: A History of the Assemblies of God.* Springfield, MO: Gospel Publishing House, 1961.

Burke, Robert. *Like A Prairie Fire: A History of the Assemblies of God in Oklahoma.* Oklahoma City: Oklahoma District Council of the Assemblies of God, 1994.

Butler, Anthea D. *Women in the Church of God in Christ: Making a Sanctified World.* Chapel Hill: University of North Carolina Press, 2007.

Campbell, Joseph E. The Pentecostal Holiness Church: Its History and Its Background. Eugene, OR: Wipf & Stock, 2016.

Clanton Arthur L., and Charles E. Clanton. *United We Stand.* Hazelwood, MO: Word Aflame Press, 1995.

Clemmons, Bishop Ithiel C. *Bishop Mason and the Roots of the Church of God in Christ.* Bakersfield, CA: Pneumalife Publishing, 1997.

Clark, Opal B. *A Fool's Enterprise: The Life of Charles Page.* Sand Springs, OK: Dexter Publishing, 2001.

Coe, Jack. *The Story Jack Coe.* Dallas, TX: Herald of Healing, 1955.

Coe, Juanita. *The Jack Coe I Know.* Dallas, TX: Herald of Healing, 1956.

Conn, Charles W. *Like a Mighty Army.* Cleveland TN: Church of God Publishing House, 1955.

Douglas, Clarence B. *The History of Tulsa, Oklahoma: A City with Personality.* Chicago: J. Clarke Publishing, 1921.

DuPree, Sherry Sherrod. *Biographical Dictionary of African-American, Holiness-Pentecostals (1880-1990)*. Washington, DC, Middle Atlantic Regional Press, 1989.

Eskelin, Neil. *The New ORU: Empowered for the 21st Century*. Tulsa, OK: Oral Roberts University.

Freestone, Jr., Orville. *Indelible Grace: An Account of Grace Pentecostal Assemblies*. Wheat Ridge, CO: Abundant Grace Fellowship, 1990.

Garrison Jack C., and Barbara Westberg. *Claiming the Land: A History of the United Pentecostal Church in the Great State of Oklahoma*. Oklahoma District United Pentecostal Church, 2012.

Gerkin, Steve. *The Hidden History of Tulsa*. Charleston, SC: History Press, 2014.

Gohr, Glenn. "A. B. and Dora Cox." *Assemblies of God Heritage* (Summer 1995): 9-11, 31

———. "An Early A/G Leader: Samuel A. Jamieson." *Assemblies of God Heritage*. (February 1991): 9-10.

———. "Raymond T. Richey, a Man with a Burning Message." *Assemblies of God Heritage* 22, no. 4 (Winter 2002-2003): 6-11.

———. "Walking by Faith, Not by Sight." *Assemblies of God Heritage* 14, no. 1 (Spring 1994): 10-13.

Goff Jr. James R., and Grant Wacker, eds. *Portraits of a Generation*. Fayetteville, AR: University of Arkansas Press, 2002.

Golder, Morris E. *History of the Pentecostal Assemblies of the World*. Indianapolis, IN: Morris E. Golder, 1973.

Goodson, Glenda Williams. "The Church of God in Christ Transforms Women's Ministries through the Positive Influence of the Chief Apostle Bishop C. H. Mason." in *With Signs Following: The Life and Ministry of Charles Harrison Mason*, edited by Raynard D. Smith, 73-96. St. Louis: Christian Board of Publication, 2015.

———. Royalty Unveiled: Women Trailblazers in the Church of God in Christ International Missions, 1920–1970. Lancaster, TX: HCM Publishing, 2011.

Goss, Ethel. *Winds of God*. New York: Comet Press Books, 1958.

Hawkins, Leroy Wesley. "A History of the Assemblies of God in Oklahoma: The Formative Years, 1914-1929." M. A. Thesis, Goodwell, OK: Panhandle State College, 1964.

Harrell, Jr., David E. All things Are Possible: The Healing & Charismatic Revivals in Modern America. Bloomington: Indian University Press, 1975.

———. *Oral Roberts: An American Life*. Bloomington, IN: Indiana University Press, 1985.

Hedges, D. J. "Pearson, Carlton Demetrius," Stanley M. Burgess and Eduard Van der Mass, eds., *New International Dictionary of Pentecostal and Charismatic Movements*. Nashville, TN: Zondervan, 2002, 959-60.

Isgrigg, Daniel D. "Healing for all Races: Oral Roberts' Legacy of Racial Reconciliation in a Divided City." *Spiritus: ORU Journal of Theology* 4, no. 9 (2019): 227-56.

———. "'I Tried Poverty': Exploring the Psychological Impact of Poverty and Prosperity in the Life of Oral Roberts." *Spiritus: ORU Journal of Theology* 5, no. 1 (2020): 5-24.

_____, "Rescued Women: Early Pentecostal Responses to Sex Trafficking," a paper presented at the 2021 annual meeting of the Society for Pentecostal Studies, South Lake, Texas, March 2021.

———., and Vinson Synan. "An Early Account of Oral Roberts' Healing Testimony." *Spiritus: ORU Journal of Theology* 3, no. 2 (2018): 168-77.

Jamieson, S. A. *Pillars of Truth*. Springfield, MO: Gospel Publishing House, 1926.

Johnson, Todd, and Gina Zurlo. *Introducing Spirit-empowered Christianity*. Tulsa, OK: ORU Press, 2020.

Kendrick, Klaude. The Promise Fulfilled: A History of the Pentecostal Movement. Springfield, MO: 1959.

King Daniel, and Daniel D. Isgrigg, "Healing En Masse." A paper presented at the Empowered21 Scholars Consultation, Tulsa, Oklahoma, June 2020.

King, J. H., *Yet Speaketh*. Franklin Springs, GA: The Publishing House of the Pentecostal Holiness Church, 1949.

Martin, Don. The First Pentecostal Church of Garden City/First Pentecostal Church of Tulsa Story. Tulsa, OK: Metro Pentecostal Church, 2003.

McClain S. D., and Robin Johnson. *Seek First the Kingdom*. Hazelwood, MO: Word Aflame Press, 2005.

McCloud, Tom, and Tara Lynn Thompson. *Journey: Tulsa's Century of Christian Faith, Leadership and Influence*. Tulsa, OK: McCloud Media, 2006.

"Oklahoma State Council 60 Years Diamond Jubilee 1958-2018," 26th Episcopal District of the Pentecostal Assemblies of the World, Oklahoma City, Oklahoma, 2018.

Osborn, T. L. *Faith Library* vol. 1. Tulsa, OK: OSFO International, 1997.

———. "My Life Story and Call to the Healing Ministry." *The Voice of Healing*, September 1949.

Paul, Harold. *Dan T. Muse: From Printer's Devil to Bishop*. Franklin Springs, GA: Advocate Press, 1976.

Prakash, Edith. Yesterday, Today, and Forever: The Extraordinary Life and Ministry of Tommy Lee Osborn. Lanham, MD: Seymour Press, 2018.

Parham, Sarah. The Life of Charles F. Parham: Founder of the Apostolic Faith Movement. Joplin, MO: The Tri-State Printing, 1930.

Robeck, Jr., Cecil M. *The Azusa Street Mission and Revival: The Birth of the Global Movement*. Nashville: Nelson Reference & Electronic, 2006.

Roberts, E. M., and Claudius Roberts. *Our Ministry and Our Son Oral*. Tulsa, OK: Oral Roberts, 1960.

Roberts, Oral. "A Spiritual Revolution Throughout the Earth." *Abundant Life*, May 1962, 6-10.

———. Expect a Miracle: My Life and My Healing Ministry. Nashville: Thomas Nelson, 1997.

———. "God Doesn't Look at Skin Color," ORU Chapel, September 26, 1989. Digital Showcase (Oral Roberts University). Accessed December 21, 2020. https://digitalshowcase.oru.edu/cgi/viewcontent.cgi?article=1008&context=chapel.

———. "God Has Spoken to me Again." *Abundant Life*, June 1960, 6-9.

———. "Great Revival at Fuquay Springs." *Pentecostal Holiness Advocate*, April 16, 1942, 13-14.

———. "My Decision to Enter the Methodist Denomination." Faculty Meeting, Oral Roberts University (March 15, 1968). Digital Showcase (Oral Roberts University) http://digitalshowcase.oru.edu/oruav/7/.

———. "My Eighteen Hours with God in Miami, Florida." *Abundant Life* 17, no. 5 (May 1963): 7.

———. "Oral Roberts Chamber of Commerce Speech." March 1, 1956, ORU Archives, accessed December 18, 2020. https://digitalshowcase.oru.edu/or_speeches/7/.

———. "Oral Roberts Meets with Bishops." Audio cassette. Holy Spirit Research Center, Oral Roberts University, Tulsa, OK, August 31, 1989. https://digitalshowcase.oru.edu/oruav/13

———. The Call: Oral Roberts Autobiography. New York: Avon Books, 1971.

———. "The Night I Found Out That God Hadn't Forgotten Me in My Struggle." *Abundant Life,* October 1979, 6-13.

———. Unleashing the Power of Praying in the Spirit. Tulsa, OK: Harrison House, 1993.

———. "Why Build A Prayer Tower." *Oral Roberts University Outreach* 3, no. 1 (Winter 1966): 7-10.

Roberts, Oral, and Larry Lea. "Going Beyond Reconciliation to Restitution." *Kingdom Lifeline*, January/February 1987, 9.

Robinson, Thomas A. *Preacher Girl: The Uldine Utley and the Industry of Revival.* Waco, TX: Baylor University Press, 2016.

Seaman, Michael. "The Emergence of Pentecostalism in Oklahoma: 1909–1930." B. A. Thesis, Stillwater, OK: Oklahoma State University, 2010.

Sims, Doris J. *Roots Out of Dry Ground: The Mother Reatha Herndon Story*. Brooklyn, NY: Welstar Publishing, 2014.

Synan, Vinson. *The Holiness-Pentecostal Movement in the United States*. Grand Rapids: Eerdmans Publishing, 1971.

———. Old Time Power: A Centennial History of the Pentecostal Holiness Church. Franklin Springs, GA: LifeSprings, 1998.

———. "Oral Roberts: Son of Pentecostalism, Father of the Charismatic Movement." *Spiritus: ORU Journal of Theology* 2, nos. 1-2 (2017): 8.

Treece, Betty. *Come to Beulah Land: The Pioneer Preacher Jerry Earl Osborn 1879-1964*. Lake Charles, LA: n.p., 1997.

Trice, Ethel. *The 70th Year Historical Souvenir Book of the Pentecostal Assemblies of the World*. Indianapolis, IN: Ethel Trice, 1985.

Tucker, Doyle. *The Mother Grace B. Tucker Story*. Tulsa, OK: Victory Publishing, 2012.

Warner, Al. "Daniel Awrey: Azusa Street Itinerant Missionary Evangelist." Paper presented at the 44th Annual Meeting of the Society for Pentecostal Studies, Lakeland, FL, March 13, 2015.

Tulsa Race Massacre History

Carson, Claybourn Ralph Luker, Penny A. Russell, and Peter Holloran, eds. *Rediscovering Precious Values*. Vol. II of *The Papers of Marin Luther King, Jr.* Berkeley: University of California Press, 1994. Excerpted from Stanford University (The Martin Luther King, Jr. Research and Education Institute). Accessed December 16, 2020. https://kinginstitute.stanford.edu/king-papers/documents/william-r-strassner.

Ellsworth, Scott. *Death in a Promised Land: The Tulsa Race Riot of 1921*. Baton Rouge: University of Louisiana Press, 1982.

———. "The Tulsa Race Riot." Tulsa Race Riot: A Report by the Oklahoma Commission to Study the Tulsa Race Riot of 1921, February 21, 2001, 49.

Fisher, Ada Lois Sipuel. *Matter of Black and White*. University of Oklahoma Press, 2006.

Franklin, John Hope and John Whittington Franklin. *My Life and An Era: The Autobiography of Buck Colbert Franklin*. Baton Rouge, LA: Louisiana State University Press, 1997.

Halliburton, Jr., R. *The Tulsa Race War of 1921*. San Francisco: R and E Research Associates, 1975.

Hirsch, James S. *Riot and Remembrance*. Boston: Houghton Mifflin, 2002.

"Inaugural Address, William Russell Strassner." *Shaw University Bulletin* 21, no. 3 (November 1951): 16-22. Accessed December 6, 2020. Excerpted from Digital NC (The North Carolina Digital Heritage Center). https://lib.digitalnc.org/record/32504

Isgrigg, Daniel D. "Healing for All Races: Oral Roberts' Legacy of Racial Reconciliation in a Divided City." *Spiritus: ORU Journal of Theology* 4, no. 2 (2019): 227-56

Johnson, Hannibal, B. *Acres of Aspiration: The All-black Towns in Oklahoma*. Austin, TX: Eakin Press, 2002.

———. Black Wallstreet: From Riot to Renaissance in Tulsa's Historic Greenwood District. Austin, TX: Eakin Press, 1998.

Keys, Alison. "East St. Louis Race Riot Left Dozens Dead and Devastating a Community on the Rise." *Smithsonian Magazine* Online, June 20, 1917. Accessed

July 5, 2020. https://www.smithsonianmag.com/smithsonian-institution/east-st-louis-race-riot-left-dozens-dead-devastating-community-on-the-rise-180963885/.

Messer Chris M. and Patricia A. Bell. "Mass Media and the Governmental Framing of Riots: The Case of Tulsa, 1921." *Journal of Black Studies* 40, no. 5 (May 2010): 851-70.

O'Dell, Larry. "Riot Property Loss." In *Tulsa Race Riot: A Report by the Oklahoma Commission to Study the Tulsa Race Riot of 1921*. Tulsa, Oklahoma: Tulsa Race Riot Commission, February 21, 2001. Oklahoma Historical Society. Accessed December 16, 2020. https://www.okhistory.org/research/forms/freport.pdf.

Parrish, Mary E. Jones. *Events of the Tulsa Disaster: An Eye-witness Account of the 1921 Tulsa Race Riot*. Mary E. Jones Parrish, 1923. Reprint., Tulsa, OK: Out on a Limb Publishing, 1998.

Tulsa Race Riot: A Report by the Oklahoma Commission to Study the Tulsa Race Riot of 1921. Tulsa, Oklahoma: Tulsa Race Riot Commission, February 21, 2001. Oklahoma Historical Society. Accessed December 16, 2020. https://www.okhistory.org/research/forms/freport.pdf.

Wattley, Cheryl Elizabeth Brown. A Step Toward Brown V. Board of Education: Ada Lois Sipuel Fisher and her Fight to End Segregation. Norman, OK: University of Oklahoma Press, 2018.

Williams, Gweneth, and Star Williams. His Story, History, and His Secret: Life through the Eyes of Otis Grandville Clark. Tulsa: Life Enrichment Publishing, 2018.

Primary Archival Sources

41st Annual Convocation: Church of God in Christ, Memphis, TN: Church of God in Christ, 1948), 23. Pentecostal and Charismatic Research Archive. Accessed December 21, 2020.

Beller, Dan. "Evangelistic Temple Church, Tulsa, Oklahoma." A paper presented to Church Growth I, Fuller Theological Seminary, Holy Spirit Research Center, Oral Roberts University, 1981.

"Business Meeting Minutes Full Gospel Tabernacle," Tulsa, Oklahoma, May 27, 1917, Flower Pentecostal Heritage Center, Springfield, MO.

Census of Religious Bodies 1926, Church of God in Christ. Department of Commerce, United States of America. Government Printing Office, 1929.

Church of God in Christ 50th Women's International Convention, Los Angeles, CA: Women's Department of Church of God in Christ, 2000, 418. USC Libraries. Accessed December 21, 2020. http://digitallibrary.usc.edu/cdm/compoundobject/collection/p15799coll14/id/115744/rec/41.

Combs, Josh, "History of First Assembly of God." October 20, 1993. Church Vertical File, Sand Springs Museum, Sand Springs, Oklahoma.

Evans, Dan W. "Historical Sketches," n.d., Dan T. Muse Papers, Holy Spirit Research Center, Oral Roberts University.

"Her Achievements." *Workshop '94: 44th State Women's Convention*. Tulsa, OK: Oklahoma Northwest Jurisdiction of the Church of God in Christ, 1994. "Annual State Women's Convention, COGIC, Tulsa, Oklahoma, 1994." USC Libraries USC Digital Library: Pentecostal and Charismatic Research Archive (PCRA). Accessed December 18, 2020. http://digitallibrary.usc.edu/cdm/compoundobject/collection/p15799coll14/id/239708/rec/16.

Muse, Dan T. "Early Pioneer Ministers of the Pentecostal Holiness Church." n.d., Dan T. Muse Papers, Holy Spirit Research Center, Oral Roberts University.

Interview with Eldoris Mae McCondiche, Tape 3, Tulsa Race Riot Survivor Stories Collection, 14 May 1999, Oklahoma Historical Society, transcript.

Interview with Eldoris Mae McCondiche, Tape 4, Tulsa Race Riot Survivor Stories Collection, 14 May 1999, Oklahoma Historical Society, transcript

"Jubilee: Vision for Victory," Sheridan Victory Christian Center, Tulsa, OK, 1981, Holy Spirit Research Center Vertical File, Tulsa, OK.

"Woodlake Assembly of God History." Woodlake Church, Bixby, Oklahoma, n.d.

Yearbook of the Church of God in Christ, Memphis, TN: 1926.

INDEX

5th and Peoria/Full Gospel Tabernacle, 26, 30-31, 41, 44, 45, 81, 84, 87-89
Adams, L. P., 27, 29
Alaman, J. L., 50, 106-108, 159
Alexander, Frank T., 11-13
Awrey, Daniel, 12-13
Azusa Street Mission, 1, 2, 7, 8, 12, 14, 65, 159

Bartlesville, OK, 10, 39-41
Bell, E. N., 12, 19, 33, 34, 35, 37, 89
Beller, Dan, 115, 116, 133
Bixby, OK, 39, 41-43, 47, 86, 116, 125, 139
Black, W. H., & Minnie 108-109, 158
Bond, Oscar. H., 20, 124
Broken Arrow, i, 26, 38, 44-46, 119, 122, 148, 150
Buckles, Edwin A., 20-21, 125
Buford Colony, 77-78

Cashwell, Gaston B. (G.B.), 9, 11, 33
Christian Chapel Assembly of God, 126-128
Church of God (Cleveland, TN), 1, 3, 33, 112
Church of God in Christ, 1 3, 5, 14-15, 20, 27, 29, 30, 48-49, 59, 60, 65, 66, 74-78, 104-108, 152, 157
Church of God of Apostolic Faith, 20-21, 124-126
Clark, Otis, 64-65, 110, 158
Coe, Jack, 129-131
Cook, Glenn, 8-9, 33, 37
Cotham, R. L., 50
Cox, A. B., 12, 16, 19

Daugherty, Billy Joe & Sharon, 123-124
Doxey, OK 8, 10-13
Duca, James, 17, 18
Duck, Arthur, 38, 98
Durham, William, 19, 33, 34

Ellis, Vep, Jr., 123, 124
Evangelistic Temple, 112-115
Faith Tabernacle, 93-94
Fire-Baptized Holiness, 7, 8, 9, 10, 12, 13

First Church of God in Christ/North Greenwood, 29, 30, 74-76, 104-105, 157
Friendship Missionary Baptist Church, 79-80
Frye, Charles O., & Vandella, 25-28, 30, 31, 34, 157

GAP Band, 105, 106
Garvin, W. F., 92, 93-95
Gaston, W. T., 19, 20, 31-32, 34, 35, 87
Goss, Howard, 17, 18, 33-34, 35, 36, 37
Greater Lansing Church of God in Christ, 76-77, 103-104
Grimes, Samuel J., 108

Hagin, Kenneth, 124, 131, 141-154
Haywood, Garfield T., 37, 52, 70
Hearne, A. L., 76-77, 103-104
Henegar, P. A., 125
Hopkins, Mary, J. 67
Herndon, Mother Reatha, 14, 15

Irwin, B. H., 7, 9

Jamieson, S. A., 32-33, 47, 49, 81, 84, 87
Jenks, 38, 39, 43, 48, 153
Jim Crow, 14, 24, 28, 61, 70, 102
Johnson, David A., 105
Jones, O. T., 14, 15

King, J. H., 2, 9, 33
Klu Klux Klan, (KKK) 114

Lamont, 8-10, 11, 13, 33
Lindsay, Charles L., 76
Lott, Harry P., 8, 9, 13

Mason, Charles H., 2, 14, 20, 27, 30, 33, 34, 59, 60, 70, 104
McCaulley, Mattie, 65-66
McCondiche, Eldoris, 62-63
McGlothen, Mattie Carter, 66-67, 158
McPherson, Aimee Semple, 3, 47, 81-85, 87, 89, 157, 159
Millard, Glenn, 88, 122-123
Moore, Oscar, 112, 113, 138

Muskogee, OK, 8, 13, 15, 16-17, 41, 119, 132

New Bethel COGIC, 78-79, 104
New Life Center/Bethel Temple, 120-122

Oklahoma City, 7, 13, 15, 103, 109, 129, 163, 165
Oneness Pentecostals, 10, 17-18, 37-38, 42, 43, 51, 52, 102, 108
Oral Roberts University, 30, 107, 110, 123, 125, 126, 138-146
Osborn, Jerry 10-11
Osborn, Ladonna, 148
Osborn, T. L. & Daisey, 107, 118, 146-148

Pearson, Carlton, 152-155
Page, Charles, 35, 48-50, 91-94
Page, E. M., 15, 17, 30, 59, 76, 103
Page Memorial Church of God in Christ, 106-107
Parham, Charles, 1, 3, 16, 19, 25-27, 31, 33-34, 44
Pentecostal Assemblies of the World, 17, 18, 37, 43, 51, 70, 102, 108-110
Pentecostal Holiness Church, 1, 13, 40, 112-113, 116, 132, 133, 141, 146
Pope, Willard, 19, 26, 31, 34, 44-46, 47, 150
Prather, Carl, 104, 105
Pringle, Steve, 113-114

Race Riot Commission, 57, 145
Richey, Raymond T., 3, 81, 90-92, 93, 94, 159
Roberts, Ellis, 132, 134, 136
Roberts, Oral, ii, 107, 112, 114, 115, 131, 132, 133, 134-146
Robinson, Lizzie, 14, 29

Sand Springs, 35, 48-50, 75, 77, 124, 136, 146, 147
Sapulpa, 17, 50-51, 66, 118, 124, 129, 130
Seymour, William, 1, 2, 8, 25, 33, 65, 70
Sipuel-Fisher, Ada Lois, 60-61, 158
Sipuel, Travis B. 17, 30, 58-59, 74
Sheridan Christian Center, 118, 122-124, 150
Strassner, William G., 49, 75-76
Still, B. L., 98-99
Sullivant, J. L., 125

Tahlequah, 8, 16, 18-21, 31
Tisdale, L. L., 79-80
Tomlinson, Ambrose J. (A.J.), 2, 112
Thompson, LaVonna, 111
Tulsa Race Massacre, ii, 3, 53-71, 73, 74, 77, 145, 158, 159

Utley, Uldine, 93

Webb, Oliver. W., 116-119
Welch, J. W., 12, 16, 17, 20, 36, 45, 90
Wicks, Mildred, 132-133
Williams, C. P., 98-99, 102
Woodlake Assembly of God, 85-86

Yandian, Bob, 11, 119, 153, 156
York, Dan & Dolly, 12, 134

www.ingramcontent.com/pod-product-compliance
Lightning Source LLC
Chambersburg PA
CBHW050318120526
44592CB00014B/1964